AN AUTHOR'S LEGACY

A planner to help your heirs and your estate.

By Craig Martelle & Audrey Hughey

Copyright © 2024 Craig Martelle and Audrey Hughey

All rights reserved. No part of this book may be reproduced without written permission from the authors.

Cover by David Berens
Editing by Mia Darien with LKJBooks.com

This is a planner for what happens when you, as the author, passes away. Did you set your heirs and your legacy up to fail? NO! Set them up for the easiest transition possible to comply with your wishes. Don't waste your life by not being prepared for death. Give yourself peace of mind and give your heirs the chance to settle your estate—we all have estates, it's simply all your worldly possessions, revenue, and debts—with the least amount of grief possible.

Although I am a lawyer, nothing in this book is to be misconstrued as legal advice. It is to help you organize your estate and ask smarter questions should you seek an estate lawyer (highly recommended) to help you draft your will, codicils, or trusts. I always advise getting a lawyer involved to help you draft a cogent and intelligent will. The will is what goes to probate, which is what gives your executor the authority to deliver to your heirs and beneficiaries according to your wishes. Don't fear probate. It's a necessary part of the process.

Also, my personal estate is in horrible disarray. I'm writing this as much for myself as I am for you. And Audrey is organizing it to make it useful for everyone, because she's great at presenting information in a way that will make sense to you.

Published by Craig Martelle, Inc
PO Box 10235
Fairbanks, AK 99710

TABLE OF CONTENTS

Identifying Data 5
Overview 6
Shared Terminology 8
Death Certificate & Immediate Death Issues 11
Your Estate 41
What Passes Within Your Estate and What Passes Outside of It? 42
Trusts 44
Your Will 46
Your Property (Everything but IP. That's later.) 50
Specific Bequests 54
Pet Care 57
Executor Duties 59
Accounts for the Executor to Consolidate Under the Estate 62
Any Codicils (Like One Designating a Literary Executor) 75
Literary Executor Duties 79
Business Plan Template (For Your Executor) 81
Author's Daily Work Routine 86
Intellectual Property (IP) 91
Author Accounts 147
People Who are Instrumental in Your Business 159
Email 175
What If You Don't Have Any Heirs? 179
Publishing Your Works-in-Progress 183
Overseas Rules 191
Resources 192
Author's Notes 193
Craig's Non-Fiction Titles 194
Audrey's Non-Fiction Titles 195

YOUR IDENTIFYING DATA

Ownership of this Document

NAME	
BIRTHDATE	
BIRTHPLACE	
SSN	
HOME ADDRESS	
SECONDARY ADDRESS	
SPOUSE/LEGAL PARTNER	
CHILDREN & BIRTHDATES	
PETS & BIRTH YEARS (IF KNOWN)	

OVERVIEW

This will be a quick overview because we don't want to belabor the fact that your life is going to end. But it's okay to plan for the next phase of your business as an author and for the benefit of your heirs. No one gets out of life alive. That's not a condemnation of your lifestyle or anything else. It is a simple fact. Of course, we try to avoid the end as long as possible, so good luck to you in living life to its fullest between the start and finish.

Someone has to settle your affairs after you pass away, so this planner is both for you to get your affairs sorted now, which will help your business grow, and most especially for your executor and those you designate to manage your intellectual property after you're gone. You can make it really hard, or you can make it easier. It'll still be hard. Settling someone's estate is never easy because of grief. This planner will help you consolidate your information and not make things more difficult after you're gone.

If you die before your non-author spouse/legal partner—I use both terms because this planner is all about what is legally defensible in a court of law—then generally, your estate will pass to them. However, are they the best person to run your author business? In many cases, that answer is no. Set your spouse up to win by ensuring that your legacy provides for them. Your books have value. Never shortchange that aspect of your life.

What about the time that precedes your death (as in, you're still alive)? Make sure you have an advanced directive in place. Go here and get one that applies to your state, as they are state specific: https://www.aarp.org/caregiving/financial-legal/free-printable-advance-directives

Wills! Everyone needs a will, and nothing in this book supersedes a will. Get one drafted in the state where you live, get your witness signatures notarized, and be done with it. If you don't take care of a will before you become incapacitated, then your heirs will suffer mightily as the State will determine what goes to whom.

If your financial planning dictates, look into life insurance. There are encyclopedias of information about choosing the right life insurance based on your situation. I recommend an internet search to get you started. Include basic information like your age, general medical health, etc.

OVERVIEW

Do you want the loan sharks to come after everything and take the entirety of your net worth after you pass? Of course you don't. Make sure the provisions of loans and other places where you have recurring costs are documented so your estate doesn't miss any payments. Who gets what after you pass? What passes within the estate and what passes outside of it (aligns more with what is taxable and what is not)?

What law applies to your situation? Authors have a tendency to be more mobile than others because we can work from anywhere. If you don't move around, that's fine. If you do, that's fine, too, but understand what laws apply to your estate once you've gone.
Intellectual property (IP)! This is the key to an author's legacy. Help your heirs to help keep your stories/books/articles alive. There is an extensive section on IP. It's not hard, but you have to instruct your heirs about things that you take for granted once you've been writing
and publishing for a while. This encompasses most of your digital assets, too. Do you have a Patreon page that earns money? Then it needs to be accounted for. And there are a million little things you do to run your business.

You don't want to make your problems your estate's problems. This planner helps you get your affairs in order, which helps you now and your heirs later. That's a win-win.

This is enough precatory language (non-binding words within a will). Let's get to the core of settling your estate.

SHARED TERMINOLOGY

The first thing to do is establish the definitions of key terms.

Decedent - That's you after you pass away, also called the deceased.

Estate – All your stuff, such as your businesses, monies, properties, and debts.

Will – The legal document that guides the management of the decedent's estate.

Intestate – When you pass away without a will. I'm here to talk you out of not doing your due diligence. Get a will!

Codicil – A legal addendum to a will.

Heir – The person who descended from the family of the decedent and is awarded a share of the estate or directly under the will. According to Cambridge, a person who will legally receive money, property, or a title from another person, especially an older member of the same family, when that other person dies.

Beneficiary – A person or entity who is designated as a recipient of a portion of the estate. This could include something like a position in a company that is outside of either money or property.

Executor – The individual who manages the directions given for the estate in the will and legal attachments and other transfer-on-death or pay-on-death instruments. The management also includes the notifications of the individual's passing, funeral arrangements, and liquidating the remaining estate for ultimate disbursement. The executor functions can be performed by more than one person—co-executors. The executor's time is billable to the estate, usually not to exceed 10% of the estate's value as a rule of thumb.

Literary Executor – A separate executor whose sole purpose is to manage the estate's intellectual property.

SHARED TERMINOLOGY

Trust / Trustee – The estate can establish a trust that will continue to receive revenue and make distributions according to instructions from the decedent. A trust can start while the decedent is still alive or after their passing. The person who administers the trust is the trustee. Trusts come in a zillion different shapes and sizes. To establish one, you need to use a lawyer skilled and experienced in setting them up.

Property – Personal, real, digital, and intellectual.

License – When it comes to intellectual property, a license grants another entity purview over works for a set amount of time and for a designated value.

Bequeath/Bequest – Arrangement for money or property to transfer after a person's death.

Probate – Your property cannot pass without a judge's order—except for spouses, usually. Probate is nothing to fear unless you don't have your ducks in a row. Make sure your ducks are in a row.

DEATH CERTIFICATE

DEATH CERTIFICATE

AND IMMEDIATE DEATH ISSUES

Your executor will put the official copy in here. Don't be morbid and think you have to do it. Leave that task for others way in your future. The executor could need anywhere from three to ten originals. When you first get them, it's easier to get a full stock in case retirement accounts or investment accounts or government agencies need an original and not a copy. I recommend ten original (raised seal) versions when you receive the first one. Simply tell the issuing agency you want ten. Pay for them out of the estate; make sure that's in your will.

Do you have any life insurance? Whole life policies or term policies. Put the information and policy number(s) here to include end dates. Put copies of the insurance certificates in this book.

PROVIDER	POLICY NUMBER	DATES	NOTES

BURIAL WISHES

Another thing to add that will help the family deal with your passing is direction to your executor regarding your burial wishes. Buried in a pine box in the veteran cemetery or cremated or something else. If you have death insurance or a prepaid burial plot, cremation, or some other disposition of your body, make sure you put those notes in here. Give your executor a fighting chance to comply with your wishes and not count on conversations you had with various family members. Under high-stress situations (like your passing away), people will have wildly varied recollections of your words. Even if they do remember correctly, it's easier and better if you have those instructions written down.

CANCELLATIONS

What will need to be canceled? These refunds are critical because they can help fund your estate account to support other costs related to your passing. Make sure you keep a calendar or planner. It can be digital, but your executor will need access to it immediately so your executor can start canceling stuff and getting refunds. Executor, use this space to identify what needs to be addressed.

In-Person Events
(Where your calendar can be found? Or just use the Calendar of Events pages.)

_____

EVENT	DATES

CANCELLATIONS

FLIGHTS
Airlines you use and login details.

AIRLINE	USERNAME	PASSWORD

HOTEL RESERVATIONS
Hotels you use and login details.

HOTEL	USERNAME	PASSWORD

CAR RENTALS
Car rental agencies you use and login details.

AGENCY	USERNAME	PASSWORD

CANCELLATIONS

CONFERENCES

NAME	WEBSITE	NOTES

IN-PERSON SALES EVENTS

NAME	DATES	CANCEL BOOK ORDER?

CALENDAR OF EVENTS

JANUARY

M	T	W	T	F	S	S
—	—	—	—	—	—	—
—	—	—	—	—	—	—
—	—	—	—	—	—	—
—	—	—	—	—	—	—
—	—	—	—	—	—	—

CALENDAR OF EVENTS

FEBRUARY

M	T	W	T	F	S	S
—	—	—	—	—	—	—
—	—	—	—	—	—	—
—	—	—	—	—	—	—
—	—	—	—	—	—	—
—	—	—	—	—	—	—

CALENDAR OF EVENTS

MARCH

M	T	W	T	F	S	S
—	—	—	—	—	—	—
—	—	—	—	—	—	—
—	—	—	—	—	—	—
—	—	—	—	—	—	—
—	—	—	—	—	—	—

_____

_____

_____

_____

CALENDAR OF EVENTS

APRIL

M	T	W	T	F	S	S
—	—	—	—	—	—	—
—	—	—	—	—	—	—
—	—	—	—	—	—	—
—	—	—	—	—	—	—
—	—	—	—	—	—	—

CALENDAR OF EVENTS

MAY

M	T	W	T	F	S	S
—	—	—	—	—	—	—
—	—	—	—	—	—	—
—	—	—	—	—	—	—
—	—	—	—	—	—	—
—	—	—	—	—	—	—

CALENDAR OF EVENTS

JUNE

M	T	W	T	F	S	S
—	—	—	—	—	—	—
—	—	—	—	—	—	—
—	—	—	—	—	—	—
—	—	—	—	—	—	—
—	—	—	—	—	—	—

CALENDAR OF EVENTS

JULY

M	T	W	T	F	S	S
—	—	—	—	—	—	—
—	—	—	—	—	—	—
—	—	—	—	—	—	—
—	—	—	—	—	—	—
—	—	—	—	—	—	—

CALENDAR OF EVENTS

AUGUST

M	T	W	T	F	S	S
—	—	—	—	—	—	—
—	—	—	—	—	—	—
—	—	—	—	—	—	—
—	—	—	—	—	—	—
—	—	—	—	—	—	—

CALENDAR OF EVENTS

SEPTEMBER

M	T	W	T	F	S	S
—	—	—	—	—	—	—
—	—	—	—	—	—	—
—	—	—	—	—	—	—
—	—	—	—	—	—	—
—	—	—	—	—	—	—

CALENDAR OF EVENTS

OCTOBER

M	T	W	T	F	S	S
—	—	—	—	—	—	—
—	—	—	—	—	—	—
—	—	—	—	—	—	—
—	—	—	—	—	—	—
—	—	—	—	—	—	—

CALENDAR OF EVENTS

NOVEMBER

M	T	W	T	F	S	S
—	—	—	—	—	—	—
—	—	—	—	—	—	—
—	—	—	—	—	—	—
—	—	—	—	—	—	—
—	—	—	—	—	—	—

CALENDAR OF EVENTS

DECEMBER

M	T	W	T	F	S	S
—	—	—	—	—	—	—
—	—	—	—	—	—	—
—	—	—	—	—	—	—
—	—	—	—	—	—	—
—	—	—	—	—	—	—

YOUR VISION

Use this section to ensure your vision for your life and authorship is clear to your heirs. What have you been striving to build? What dreams have you been working toward achieving?

YOUR VISION

Why is writing important to you? Why is it such a crucial part of who you are and your life's vision? How does it help define the legacy you wish to leave?

YOUR VISION

What is the most important thing you want your heirs to know about your writing and what it means to you?

YOUR PLANS

YOUR TOP 3 GOALS & MILESTONES

GOAL 1:

Milestone Step to Achievement	Deadline/Target

Notes

_____

_____

_____

YOUR PLANS

GOAL 2:	
Milestone Step to Achievement	Deadline/Target

Notes

YOUR PLANS

GOAL 3:	
Milestone Step to Achievement	Deadline/Target

Notes
_____
_____
_____
_____

YOUR PLANS

MOST IMPORTANT PROJECTS			
Priority	PROJECT	Deadline / Target	Notes

YOUR PLANS

QUARTER 1: GOALS, EVENTS, TASKS, PROJECTS, & DEADLINES

Priority	ITEM	Deadline / Target	Notes

Notes

_____

_____

_____

_____

YOUR PLANS

QUARTER 2: GOALS, EVENTS, TASKS, PROJECTS, & DEADLINES			
Priority	ITEM	Deadline / Target	Notes

Notes

_____
_____
_____
_____

YOUR PLANS

QUARTER 3: GOALS, EVENTS, TASKS, PROJECTS, & DEADLINES			
Priority	ITEM	Deadline / Target	Notes

Notes
_____
_____
_____
_____

YOUR PLANS

QUARTER 4: GOALS, EVENTS, TASKS, PROJECTS, & DEADLINES

Priority	ITEM	Deadline / Target	Notes

Notes

_____
_____
_____
_____

YOUR PLANS

Any remaining notes to share regarding your plans, visions, or goals?

YOUR ESTATE

WHAT TRANSFERS?

What passes within your estate and what passes outside of it?

I wish this was straightforward, but it is not. There are more taxes than you can shake a stick at in the United States and in individual states in particular.

Estate taxes are levied on the net value of an estate before distribution. (The threshold is usually in the millions and applies in few cases.)

Inheritance tax (also called death tax) is a tax on the transfer of wealth to the beneficiaries. This is also usually limited to high-dollar values. Your probate lawyer will be able to answer questions about the thresholds as they apply to your state. This is a state-only tax and not federal.

Transfer-on-death (TOD, also called pay-on-death, POD) transfers outside of probate and relatively quickly after the financial institution is provided evidence that the owner has passed away.
- **Certificates of deposit (CDs)** transfer outside the estate but only new interest earned is taxable. The principal generally transfers tax-free.
- **Individual Retirement Accounts (IRAs) or 401k accounts** are taxed based on whether taxes have already been paid or not. Roth IRAs pass tax-free because they were purchased with taxable income. Traditional IRAs were deducted from pre-tax dollars and will be taxed upon the transfer unless the recipient rolls them into a new IRA where you'll probably get charged "maintenance" costs.
- **Other tax-deductible retirement and investment contributions** will probably be taxed, and the effect on the beneficiary could be extreme, bumping them into a higher tax bracket on all their taxable income in the year that they took the payment from the deceased's account.

Note these assets in the Accounts section of this planner

WHAT TRANSFERS?

Accounts solely in the deceased's (your) name without a transfer on death provision (your average checking and savings accounts are usually like this) will be ordered transferred by a probate judge. No one can transfer your property without legal authority. Your vehicle that is solely in your name? The judge gives the estate authority over the vehicle so it can be sold/transferred.

Avoid the limbo of intellectual property. If you do nothing with it, it will eventually stop earning and be relatively worthless, but never forget, your words have value, and you can always sell a good book. Make sure your literary executor is able to dive in right away and keep the revenue train churning. It'll take some effort, depending on how well you've set things up. Give them a chance to keep putting your work in front of the right readers.

> Use this space to record any questions you may have for a legal professional regarding the transfer of your assets.

TRUSTS

These are extremely complex, and every trust is written very specifically for the recipient of the trust's disbursements.

Trusts can be started while you're still alive, such as a living trust, revocable and irrevocable trusts, annuities, and many more.

Trusts can be activated after you pass away. You set the conditions for these in your will. This is a testamentary trust. The big drawback to these is you have to count on your executor to make sure it's set up properly to deliver the result you're looking for. If you want one to manage your IP, then who are the trustees? Are they wise in the way of publishing? Set yourself up to win and establish the trust before you pass away, even if it doesn't get funded until afterward. You'll know that it will accede to your wishes.

You can set up other trusts in your will. I have a literary trust in mine that will be set up to manage my IP. I should probably make that a living trust that I start funding now with a percentage of my business proceeds. I want annuities to my wife and son from this trust. Easy enough to establish that now. So why haven't I? Trusts are hard, and they can be expensive. I'm a lawyer but will have to pay another lawyer to do this for me because I don't know jack about establishing a trust beyond basic nomenclature. There's no reason to delay besides procrastinating. I challenge myself to get this done before this planner is finalized for publication.

My emphasis here is about hiring the right person. You can find trust kits online, but they cannot deal appropriately with everything that applies to your particular situation to set up a trust correctly and in a way that benefits your heirs. You think you might be able to defer setting up the trust because you may not have the money now. If you pass away without any money to fund your estate plans, then how will your executor set up a trust? They won't be able to, even though your IP could take off years after your death. If the trust doesn't get established, what are you going to do about it? Not a damn thing. You won't be there. Some ex-spouse of a distance relative will be suing for control of what could be a fortune, or worse, your IP disappears into obscurity because no one knows it exists.

Establish your trust in the right way and have it ready to go. Like the man said, "It's the only way to be sure."

TRUSTS

Use this space to record any questions you may have for a legal professional regarding trusts.

YOUR WILL

Put a copy of your will in this section. No matter what is in this book, the legal instrument to set up your estate for success is your will.

Make sure you include these elements within your will:
- The will applies to the state in which you live because each state has slightly different laws regarding estates and succession. Make sure it complies with state law. (Get an estate lawyer.)
- Personal information, so there's no doubt this is you and that this is your last will and testament.
- Designate an executor and a secondary in case the first cannot carry out the duties of executor. As a side note, designate an executor who will not be emotionally destroyed by your passing. The executor has far too many duties to perform if he/she is inconsolable and a complete wreck.
- Designate your heirs and alternates, in case the first predeceases you.
- Detail the distribution of your estate—the remainder after debts are paid—and ensure you designate either per stirpes (by the branch, where one share to a child is one share, even if that child dies before you, as their heirs will get their one share) or per capita (separate shares as if they were your children, which is different).
- Note from where your debts will be paid, which is usually "my estate."
- Property and assets
- Guardianship (account for your minor children and pets)
- Sign the will. It's best if you get two notarized signatures testifying that it was you who signed the will. This is called self-attesting and makes probate much easier. (Witnesses only attest that it was you who signed, not that they know the content of the will.)

If you want to establish a trust that activates after you pass away, that is called a testamentary trust and can be changed any time before you pass away. A revocable trust is one that you start before you pass away. An irrevocable trust can also be started before you pass away. There are different tax implications based on revocability, which comes with the level of control you exert while you're still alive as a grantor or non-grantor. Trusts are complex but serve a critical purpose after you're gone in providing a revenue stream to a designee(s) in a formal way. Consult a professional to establish said trust and make sure they understand the implications of intellectual property when establishing trusts that are funded with them, as part of a coordinated estate plan.

What do you do if you don't have heirs? There's a chapter in the book on that.

YOUR WILL

You can use this planner (An Author's Legacy) to help you draft your will and even list this book as an addendum to it that will help your executor comply with your wishes for your estate.

Here's a simple will as a bare bones example, just to give you an idea. It's best if you see an estate lawyer. Pay the small fee and have the will drafted properly and as precisely as you desire.

Once you have your signature on your will witnessed, you'll want to protect it. Keep it (and this planner) in a fire-resistant safe or a safe-deposit box. Make sure someone else has access to any safe-deposit box. maybe your executor has a key and is named for access with the bank. If you bury this will in a safe in the woods, then make sure someone knows where and has the safe combination. When your executor goes before the probate judge, he or she will need to provide a copy of the will and any attachments for validation and verification. (This is where the notarized will makes things easier.)

Use this space to record any questions you may have for a legal professional regarding the writing of your will.

_____
_____
_____
_____
_____
_____
_____
_____
_____
_____

SAMPLE WILL

Simple Will (Sample)

I, _____ (name), resident of _____ (city and state), declare that this is my final Will and Testament. I hereby revoke all prior Wills.

1. I give [insert description of gifts of property, money, etc., or a simple gift (such as "my entire estate to _____, if he/she survives me, or if not, to _____") or a fractional gift (such as "one-half of my entire estate")].

2. I nominate _____ as executor of my Will, to serve without bond.

3. Notwithstanding any other provision of this Will, after my death, my executor shall not distribute any part of my estate consisting of (a) ideas, manuscripts, books, drawings, pictures, scripts, playscripts, treatments, stories, poetry, dramas, or any other fiction or nonfiction writings, whether published or unpublished, created in whole or in part by me (collectively "Writings"), (b) rights to proceeds from any Writings, rights to publish, exploit, license, or sell any Writings, contracts for the publication, exploitation, licensing, or sale of any Writings, and any derivative or secondary rights in or to the Writings or derived from the Writings, as well as (c) rights to any performances, recordings, readings, or dramatizations by me and my name and likeness (collectively "Creative Property"), but instead shall transfer all of the Creative Property to the special trustees named in this Will, to hold in trust in perpetuity (to be known as the "Creative Property Trust"), as follows:

A. The special trustees shall, in addition to those powers now or hereafter conferred by law or by the other terms of this Will, solely and exclusively have the following powers with respect to the Creative Property:

SAMPLE WILL

(1) To publish, exploit, license, and sell, in the special trustees' sole discretion, any Writings;

(2) To retain any Writings and refrain from publishing, exploiting, licensing, or selling such Writings for as long as the special trustees deem appropriate, at the risk of the trust estate, in the special trustees' discretion.

B. Notwithstanding any other designation of the trustee or trustees in this Will, after my death, _____, _____, and _____ shall serve as special trustees of the Creative Property Trust. If any of them fails to qualify or ceases to act as a special trustee, the remaining of them shall designate a successor trustee to serve in his or her place as a special trustee of the Creative Property Trust.

C. All income and principal of the Creative Property Trust (other than Creative Property) shall be distributed immediately upon receipt to _____.

Executed at _____, on _____, 20___.

_____

WITNESSED:
_____
_____

WITNESSED:
_____
_____

YOUR PROPERTY

Your Property (Everything but IP. That's later.)

Spreadsheet – An Author's Legacy - https://geni.us/AnAuthorsLegacy

You'll have to download the file to the type of your choice, like Google Sheets or Excel. This file can only be viewed via Google. Also, please do not share this spreadsheet – it is exclusively for the use of those who bought this planner.

REAL PROPERTY: REAL ESTATE

Real Property - Type: _____

Address: _____

Ownership Level (co-owned, owned outright, still owe, etc.): _____

Notes: _____

Real Property - Type: _____

Address: _____

Ownership Level: _____

Notes: _____

Real Property - Type: _____

Address: _____

Ownership Level: _____

Notes: _____

YOUR PROPERTY

Post Office Box (possibly for your author business)**:** _____

Address: _____

Billed monthly/annually? _____ Amount: _____

Autopayment from which account? _____

Notes: _____

Physical Property

Make sure if you sell an item listed below, you cross it off so your executor doesn't go crazy looking for it. I suggest these items have a value of at least a few thousand dollars (car, boat, 1952 Willy Mays Rookie Card, etc.).

Physical Property	Est. Value	Location / Notes

YOUR PROPERTY

Physical Property	Est. Value	Location / Notes

YOUR PROPERTY

Physical Property	Est. Value	Location / Notes

SPECIFIC BEQUESTS

Do you have particular items that you want to go to particular people? It's not hard to list the item(s) and the person. Help your executor to help you.

I expect, like most authors, you have your personal collection of physical books—those you've read and those you've written. Take care to list who those go to specifically, whether a library, individual, charity, or whatever, so the collection can stay intact.

ITEM	TO WHOM

SPECIFIC BEQUESTS

ITEM	TO WHOM

SPECIFIC BEQUESTS

ITEM	TO WHOM

PET CARE

Do you have a pet or pets? What will happen to them after you're gone? The bad news is if someone doesn't immediately step up to take care of them, they'll go to the pound. Please don't do that to your beloved friends. You can use residual funds from your estate to pay expenses for the animals' care.

Make the guidance generic enough that it accounts for any pets that come into or out of your life and are present at the time of your passing. Something like this could suffice.

"From my Literary Trust, food and veterinarian services will be paid for the animals currently living in my house or under my care for the rest of their lives."

Is there any other information on your pets you'd like to share, such as food foibles, allergies, vet, etc.?

_____
_____
_____
_____
_____
_____
_____
_____
_____
_____
_____
_____
_____

PET CARE

EXECUTOR DUTIES

EXECUTOR DUTIES

The executor may have to drop a lot of what is going on in their lives in order to perform the duties of an executor.

An executor of a will is responsible for carrying out the deceased's wishes as outlined in the will, and for closing out the deceased's affairs. This includes many duties, such as:

- Notifying parties
- Informing beneficiaries, heirs, creditors, and government agencies of the death
- Filing paperwork
- Filing the will with the probate court, and other documents as required
- Managing assets
- Creating an inventory of the estate's assets, and maintaining property until it can be sold or distributed
- Paying debts and taxes, which includes establishing an estate account. That means you'll need to get an EIN, and you can't do that online. Get a probate lawyer and that individual, in conjunction with a local bank, will help you make it happen. This further includes funeral and burial expenses, medical bills, and credit card debt. Filing taxes if necessary.
- Distributing assets
- Making timely distributions of assets to the beneficiaries named in the will
- Representing the estate
- Deciding what type of probate is needed, and representing the estate in court
- Keeping beneficiaries informed
- Providing accountings to interested parties, and keeping beneficiaries updated on estate-related decisions

That's an extensive list of full-time work if the decedent isn't squared away. That's what this planner is all about. Don't try to fill it out in one sitting. That would be exhausting. Think about your heirs while doing it a little at a time. Continue to build your legacy by writing and publishing, and cement your legacy by leaving a record behind for others to follow.

If you're a veteran, your executor will be responsible for notifying the Veterans Administration. Call 1-800-827-1000 (TTY: 711) and select 5, Monday through Friday, 8 AM–9 PM, Eastern time.

EXECUTOR DUTIES

Notify the Social Security Administration.

The executor will arrange the decedent's final taxes. To do that, the executor needs access to your revenue and expenses. Are you keeping track? All of mine is in a spreadsheet that my accountant has access to. That's the easiest way to do things. My accountant is my niece, who I trust implicitly. Find someone you can trust to that level and give them access. Make the executor's job easier.

Use this space to record any questions you may have for a legal professional regarding executor duties.

_____
_____
_____
_____
_____
_____
_____
_____
_____
_____
_____
_____
_____
_____
_____

ACCOUNTS TO CONSOLIDATE

Accounts for the Executor to Consolidate Under the Estate

Note if any of these are TOD/POD (transfer-on-death or pay-on-death, which transfer outside the estate).

Spreadsheet – An Author's Legacy - https://geni.us/AnAuthorsLegacy

You'll have to download the file to the type of your choice, like Google Sheets or Excel. This file can only be viewed via Google. Also, please do not share this spreadsheet – it is exclusively for the use of those who bought this planner.

Use this space to record any questions you may have for a legal professional regarding the consolidation of your accounts.

_____
_____
_____
_____
_____
_____
_____
_____
_____
_____
_____

ACCOUNTS TO CONSOLIDATE

CREDITS

Bank / Credit Union:

Account	Account #s	Owner(s)	PINs / Passwords	Notes

Bank / Credit Union:

Account	Account #s	Owner(s)	PINs / Passwords	Notes

ACCOUNTS TO CONSOLIDATE

CREDITS

Bank / Credit Union:				
Account	Account #s	Owner(s)	PINs / Passwords	Notes

Bank / Credit Union:				
Account	Account #s	Owner(s)	PINs / Passwords	Notes

ACCOUNTS TO CONSOLIDATE

INVESTMENTS

Investment Bank:

Type	Account #s	Owner(s)	PINs / Passwords	Notes

Investment Bank:

Type	Account #s	Owner(s)	PINs / Passwords	Notes

ACCOUNTS TO CONSOLIDATE

INVESTMENTS

Investment Bank:

Type	Account #s	Owner(s)	PINs / Passwords	Notes

Investment Bank:

Type	Account #s	Owner(s)	PINs / Passwords	Notes

ACCOUNTS TO CONSOLIDATE

INVESTMENTS

401k/SEP/IRA:				
Account #	Owner(s)	PINs / Passwords	Managed by:	Notes

401k/SEP/IRA:				
Account #	Owner(s)	PINs / Passwords	Managed by:	Notes

ACCOUNTS TO CONSOLIDATE

INVESTMENTS

401k/SEP/IRA:

Account #	Owner(s)	PINs / Passwords	Managed by:	Notes

401k/SEP/IRA:

Account #	Owner(s)	PINs / Passwords	Managed by:	Notes

ACCOUNTS TO CONSOLIDATE

INVESTMENTS

Stocks owned that were purchased directly. Attach stock certificates or printouts showing share ownership; a quarterly statement will do.

Account	Owner(s)	PINs / Passwords	Transfer on Death?	If so, to whom?

ACCOUNTS TO CONSOLIDATE

DEBTS

MORTGAGES					
Lender	Account #	PINs / Passwords	Payment Due Date	Amount	Account Paid From

Notes

_____
_____
_____
_____
_____
_____

ACCOUNTS TO CONSOLIDATE

DEBTS

\multicolumn{6}{c}{**Other Loans.** Vehicles, personal, etc.}
Lender	Account #	PINs / Passwords	Payment Due Date	Amount	Account Paid From

Notes

_____
_____
_____
_____

ACCOUNTS TO CONSOLIDATE

DEBTS

Other Debts. Credit cards, etc.					
Creditor	**Account #**	**PINs / Passwords**	**Payment Due Date**	**Amount**	**Account Paid From**

Notes

_____

_____

_____

_____

ACCOUNTS TO CONSOLIDATE

DEBTS

Other Debts. Credit cards, etc.					
Creditor	Account #	PINs / Passwords	Payment Due Date	Amount	Account Paid From

Notes

EXPENSES

If you have receipts stuffed into a folder or piled in a closet, you need to rethink your life choices. Be better than that, because if you miss a valid deductible, the IRS will happily take your money that you might not need to pay.

Your Executor fills in your estate account information, you fill in everything above. The Executor will have to switch recurring credits and debits from real estate and other accounts that need to remain active to this account from the previous pages so those can be incrementally closed out.

Estate Bank Account: _____

Account Number: _____

Account EIN: _____

Account Owner (exact name on account): _____

Notes: _____

_____

_____

_____

_____

_____

_____

_____

_____

_____

_____

_____

CODICILS

CODICILS

Any Codicils (Like One Designating a Literary Executor)

Put a copy of the codicils in here. Until you get a proper one, you can annotate this one to get you started, but you'll still need to get it witnessed to validate it.

Here's a sample codicil designating a literary executor.

CODICIL to the Last Will & Testament of [name]

[date]

I, [name], a resident of the County of [county], State of [state], declare that this is the codicil to my last will and testament, which is dated [date original signed].

I add or change said last will in the following manner:

I appoint _____ to be the literary executor of my estate, hereinafter referred to as my "Literary Executor"), to have custody of, act with respect to, and be empowered to make all determinations concerning the use, disposition, retention, and control of the literary works that I have created or own, my letters, correspondence, documents, private papers, writings, manuscripts, and all other literary property of any kind created by me, whether or not any such items are unfinished or are completed but not yet divulged to the public. Should a dispute arise between the Literary Executor and General Executor concerning my literary property, the determination of the General Executor shall be final and binding.

Should the above-named individual predecease me, then I appoint _____ to be the literary executor.

My literary properties and ownership details, known to me at this time are as follows (but not limited to):

CODICILS

Author Name & series titles (include individual works if you wish, plus initial copyright date).

Author Name & Collaborator Name (note the ownership share of the works and initial copyright date).

Pen Name & series titles (include validation that this is your pen name, copyright date, and any collaborators and their share if they receive one).

I have granted rights in my works as follows.
List works under license and the license details (to whom, dates inclusive, other contracts). Also include whether to extend the license or not, should I predecease the license end date.

If you want to bequeath a specific title to someone, then you would do that with the following clause.

I give and bequeath all my right, title, and interest, including but limited to all rights under copyrights and all other intellectual property rights in my manuscript entitled _____ to _____ (son, daughter, bestest buddy, whatever), if he/she shall survive. If not, then this work shall be added to my general literary estate for disposition as determined by my Literary Executor according to my directions herein.

For as long as my copyrights remain in effect, the Literary Executor shall make every effort to promote my literary works through digital, paper, media, and other formats not yet established or contemplated. The copyrights are to inure to the benefit of my heirs through monies earned and paid through the General Executor. For this continued effort, the Literary Executor may retain up to twenty five percent (25%) of the annual profit for himself/herself. The Literary Executor may use up to ten percent (10%) of the revenue from my literary properties for promotional and advertising purposes. Sums outside this amount must be approved by my General Executor.

Otherwise, I hereby confirm and republish my will dated [date original signed], in all respects other than those herein mentioned.

CODICILS

I subscribe my name to this codicil this *[day, e.g. 1st]* day of *[month]*, *[year]*, at *[full address where signed]*, in the presence of *[full name of first witness to codicil]*, *[full name of second witness to codicil]*, and *[full name of third witness to codicil]*, attesting witnesses, who subscribe their names here in my presence .

_____
Maker

ATTEST

On the date last above written, *[name]*, known by us to be the person whose signature appears at the end of this codicil, declared to us, *[full name of first witness to codicil]*, *[full name of second witness to codicil]*, and *[full name of third witness to codicil]*, the undersigned, that the foregoing instrument, consisting of *[number of pages to codicil]* page(s) was the codicil to the will dated *[date original signed]*, who then signed the codicil in our presence, and now in the presence of each other, we now sign our names as witnesses.

_____
Witness

Address:
_____
_____
_____

_____
Witness

Address:
_____
_____
_____

LITERARY EXECUTOR DUTIES

LITERARY EXECUTOR DUTIES

The literary executor is responsible for managing the deceased's IP to continue earning revenue and staying relevant in the literary world, including finding new readers and keeping the properties earning.

Those are simple but extremely difficult. The literary executor becomes the CEO of your intellectual property, your published and unpublished works in all their formats, and continues their presentation to the reading public (readers of your genre(s) and more).

The executor is responsible for notifying Amazon and other distributors of the author's death. Some of the distributors will transfer the title to a new account established by the literary executor for the purposes of these duties, which keeps the IP separate from the literary executor's. I assume the literary executor is published and knows what they're doing in the publication and marketing of IP when they receive access to the account where the IP is promulgated and most importantly, the latest and greatest versions of every single book.

Who do you leave your copyrights to? This is probably the hardest question, as demonstrated by Ernest Hemingway's estate. I recommend bloodline specific with complete copyrights designated. Don't split a copyright, or even better, put them into a trust to manage to inure to the benefit of your blood relations. Why blood? So a grandchild's ex-spouse can't get control of your work because of a bitter divorce. Or great-grandchild, and so on.

What do you do on a daily basis to manage your work? Include your daily work plan or level of effort. The next few sections deal with you and how you run your business. Your executor won't be able to replicate it in total, but they can prioritize to keep the revenue flowing.

What about physical mail related to your business? You'll need the executor to make sure you get it or copies of it, depending on what "it" is. Keep in mind that any newsletters will have a valid mailing address. It could be a post office box. Make sure you account for that and forward the mail to the executor/literary executor based on exclusivity of what goes to the box.

BUSINESS PLAN

Business Plan Template for Your Executor

WHAT + HOW + WHO	WHAT do we do?	
	HOW do we do it?	
	WHO do we serve?	
WHY	DEFINE CUSTOMER PROBLEM	
	DEFINE SOLUTION PROVIDED	
REVENUE	PRICING & BILLING STRATEGIES	
	INCOME STREAMS	
MARKETING	CUSTOMER RESEARCH STRATEGY	
	REFERRAL GENERATION STRATEGY	
VISION	STORIES IN FOCUS	
	TOTAL TITLES	
METRICS	SUCCESS MILESTONE MARKER 1	
	SUCCESS MILESTONE MARKER 2	

BUSINESS PLAN

Business Plan Template for Your Executor

	INTERNAL FACTORS	
SITUATIONAL ANALYSIS (SWOT)	**STRENGTHS (+)**	**WEAKNESSES (-)**
	EXTERNAL FACTORS	
	OPPORTUNITIES (+)	**THREATS (-)**

BUSINESS PLAN

Use this space for explanations of important aspects of the business plan above or more in-depth conversations about your business.

_____
_____
_____
_____
_____
_____
_____
_____
_____
_____
_____
_____
_____
_____
_____
_____
_____
_____
_____

BUSINESS PLAN

Use this space for explanations of important aspects of the business plan above or more in-depth conversations about your business.

BUSINESS PLAN

Use this space for explanations of important aspects of the business plan above or more in-depth conversations about your business.

WORK ROUTINE

Author's Daily Work Routine

WRITE NEW WORDS Hours, word count, or both.	
EDIT OLD WORDS	
WIPS: **WORKS IN PROGRESS** This will change frequently. Maybe just point to where these files or lists reside on your computer along with any active series you continue to add to.	
IN-PERSON EVENTS Where can your schedule for in-person events be found, so they can be canceled after you pass?	
ADVERTISING REVIEW Explain your process.	
SET UP FUTURE PROMOTIONS	

WORK ROUTINE

MANAGE ASSISTANTS	
SOCIAL MEDIA How much time and what.	
NEWSLETTER Information (what lists to which readers, where do your subs come from, etc.)	
ANSWER EMAILS	
COORDINATE / COLLABORATE	
PATREON Or other subscription platforms.	

WORK ROUTINE

VIDEOS YOU'VE MADE

BLOG POSTS
Or other IP you've created in odd places.

WORK ROUTINE

Any final notes on your business.

WORK ROUTINE

Any final notes on your business.

INTELLECTUAL PROPERTY

INTELLECTUAL PROPERTY (IP)

As an author, both established and new, you probably have little grasp of how far your work has reached. Each touch point is something to be managed. When you're gone, you can no longer handle things with a simple email or message. You know all the background. Your executor or literary executor will have to research every issue. How painful can this be? Extremely, and the easiest answer is to err on the side of caution, so IP will grow stagnant over time. That's better than losing the IP to opportunists or outright scammers who buy it for pennies on the dollar. Copyright is one form of protection of your creation.

Here's the copyright office's definition of copyright.

> *Copyright is a type of intellectual property that protects **original works of authorship** as soon as an author **fixes** the work in a **tangible form of expression**. In copyright law, there are a lot of different types of works, including paintings, photographs, illustrations, musical compositions, sound recordings, computer programs, books, poems, blog posts, movies, architectural works, plays, and so much more!*

Intellectual property is anything you've created. You can sue someone if they infringe on your copyright. Sometimes, you'll want to register your work with the U.S. Copyright Office (https://www.copyright.gov), which gives you the ability to collect damages, costs, and more if you have to sue a disreputable individual/company.

Important safety tip: NEVER sell your copyright, only license it. And now that you've passed, the seventy-year clock starts the countdown to the end of your copyright protection.

Copyrights will be the most difficult part of your estate. If you have any success, your heirs could start a big, ugly fight over control. Don't let your copyrights get split between people. That has the potential to destroy their value. I strongly recommend a literary trust that manages the properties and disburses revenue therefrom. In my will, I turn over many co-authored properties to my co-author if they did the majority of the writing on the book(s), so my overall portfolio will be reduced, but it is still substantial, and the most valuable IP remains in my control.

If you don't want a trust, then be very specific about your copyrights. Maybe you only want them to go to blood relatives like your own children and their progeny. By declaring blood relatives only, no former spouses will ever have a claim on your IP. Your will determines who controls the IP through the end of your copyright (death plus seventy years) and beyond. I recommend M.L. Ronn's excellent discussion of the subject in his The Author Estate Handbook.

Keeping track of your IP can become a full-time job for someone who is picking up the pieces after you're gone. Don't do that to them! There's a form on the next page to write down the pertinent information for each title or series, depending on your body of work, but it would be even better in a spreadsheet, because over time, you will create a great volume of IP. Use the cool spreadsheet for both ease of access and to be more complete and up-to-date.

INTELLECTUAL PROPERTY (IP)

If you've written one book, you'll sell it in every form you can, appealing to however a buyer consumes their entertainment—ebook, paperback, hardcover, audiobook, translations, graphic novel, and eventually, direct injection into a consumer's brain (or in new contract language, in mediums not yet devised or contemplated). Each one of those is a separate property based on your initial IP.

There are identification numbers (ISBN, ASIN, copyright cert, and so many more) that apply to each form of your work. There are contracts (cover, artwork, secondary distribution). There could be licensing (art, distribution, royalty share), options (for television or movies). The channels and interactions are numerous. Put the information in one place and make it easier on the person who will take over your publishing empire.

Translations are a unique piece of IP, separate from the original, as is each audiobook version, graphic novel version, merchandise, derivative rights, and more. You own copyright on the story and characters. You can also trademark a series or characters, but that's a different and costly process that most authors don't undertake. If you have any questions, refer to the https://www.uspto.gov/trademarks.

Your book files are critical for extending your legacy. New opportunities may require the source files—your books, covers, and metadata. Keeping that stuff organized will make your heir or heirs' lives better.

I was able to copy the hard drive of a deceased author's computer so I could write the last two books in his series. Even with that, I had significant challenges. He wrote on a Mac, not a PC like me, so I had some file conversions to do. I also had to find the source files for each book, which were in multiple places. There were less than twenty books, but consolidating, verifying, and reestablishing each series and each book took some time. Add in a couple quality issues on Amazon's bookshelf, and I had my hands full ensuring the legacy continued. I added two books to the series, and they were well received by nearly all the readers. I had notes for book five and had only the cover and title for book six. No one can write your books like you, but someone may have to try in order to do you a favor and complete a series.

The Google spreadsheet is an additional source of information where you can copy/paste book links and that stuff along with all the important data and contacts, like the cover designer or narrator. You can also handwrite the info here. Give your heirs a chance to succeed and keep your books alive.

Spreadsheet: An Author's Legacy - https://geni.us/AnAuthorsLegacy

You'll have to download the file to the type of your choice, like Google Sheets or Excel. This file can only be viewed via Google. Also, please do not share this spreadsheet – it is exclusively for the use of those who bought this planner.

BOOK INFORMATION

The following pages provide space to record a laundry list of information related to your titles, one page for each or one page for each series. It would be best if you put this information in a spreadsheet.

Spreadsheet – An Author's Legacy - https://geni.us/AnAuthorsLegacy

You'll have to download the file to the type of your choice, like Google Sheets or Excel. This file can only be viewed via Google. Also, please do not share this spreadsheet – it is exclusively for the use of those who bought this planner.

Use this space and the next page to record any additional notes about your books that you'd like to leave for your executor.

_____
_____
_____
_____
_____
_____
_____
_____
_____
_____
_____
_____
_____

BOOK INFORMATION

BOOK INFORMATION

BOOK TITLE/SERIES:	
Book # in Series:	Check here if standalone: ☐
Published by:	
Are you paid by a publisher or do you pay a co-author?	
Co-Author Name:	Co-Author Email:
Co-Author Share %:	Frequency of Payments: (Monthly/Quarterly/Annually)
Co-Author Contract Location (Include a copy on the hard drive with the most up-to-date copy of this book including the cover and metadata, like the blurb.):	

Cover Artist:	Email:	Date:
Typography by:	Email:	
Editing by:	Email:	Date:

ISBN:	Format (ebook/audio/paperback/hard cover)	Personal/Amazon/Ingram/Publisher/etc.:
ISBN:	Format (ebook/audio/paperback/hard cover)	Personal/Amazon/Ingram/Publisher/etc.:
ISBN:	Format (ebook/audio/paperback/hard cover)	Personal/Amazon/Ingram/Publisher/etc.:
ISBN:	Format (ebook/audio/paperback/hard cover)	Personal/Amazon/Ingram/Publisher/etc.:
Translation Language:	Translator + Contact:	ISBN + Source:
Translation Language:	Translator + Contact:	ISBN + Source:
Translation Language:	Translator + Contact:	ISBN + Source:

Audiobook Narrator:	Email:	
Amazon ASIN:	B&N ebook:	Apple ebook:
Kobo ebook:	Other:	Other:
Direct Sale Location/Link:		

BOOK INFORMATION

Audiobook Channel:	Date Added:
Audiobook Channel:	Date Added:
Audiobook Channel:	Date Added:
Audiobook Channel:	Date Added:
Audiobook Channel:	Date Added:
Audiobook Channel:	Date Added:
If you have the title optioned for film, put that information here -- who, contact info, and date option ends.	
Are there licenses in your digital folders for anything here? These include licenses for cover artwork, distribution, audio, and anything else that requires a license:	

ANY OTHER INFORMATION THAT'S UNIQUE TO THIS TITLE/SERIES?

_____
_____
_____
_____
_____
_____
_____
_____
_____
_____
_____
_____
_____

BOOK INFORMATION

BOOK TITLE/SERIES:	
Book # in Series:	Check here if standalone: ☐
Published by:	
Are you paid by a publisher or do you pay a co-author?	
Co-Author Name:	Co-Author Email:
Co-Author Share %:	Frequency of Payments: (Monthly/Quarterly/Annually)
Co-Author Contract Location (Include a copy on the hard drive with the most up-to-date copy of this book including the cover and metadata, like the blurb.):	
Cover Artist:	Email:	Date:
Typography by:	Email:	
Editing by:	Email:	Date:
ISBN:	Format (ebook/audio/paperback/hard cover)	Personal/Amazon/Ingram/Publisher/etc.:
ISBN:	Format (ebook/audio/paperback/hard cover)	Personal/Amazon/Ingram/Publisher/etc.:
ISBN:	Format (ebook/audio/paperback/hard cover)	Personal/Amazon/Ingram/Publisher/etc.:
ISBN:	Format (ebook/audio/paperback/hard cover)	Personal/Amazon/Ingram/Publisher/etc.:
Translation Language:	Translator + Contact:	ISBN + Source:
Translation Language:	Translator + Contact:	ISBN + Source:
Translation Language:	Translator + Contact:	ISBN + Source:
Audiobook Narrator:	Email:	
Amazon ASIN:	B&N ebook:	Apple ebook:
Kobo ebook:	Other:	Other:
Direct Sale Location/Link:		

BOOK INFORMATION

Audiobook Channel:	Date Added:
Audiobook Channel:	Date Added:
Audiobook Channel:	Date Added:
Audiobook Channel:	Date Added:
Audiobook Channel:	Date Added:
Audiobook Channel:	Date Added:

If you have the title optioned for film, put that information here -- who, contact info, and date option ends.

Are there licenses in your digital folders for anything here? These include licenses for cover artwork, distribution, audio, and anything else that requires a license:

ANY OTHER INFORMATION THAT'S UNIQUE TO THIS TITLE/SERIES?

_____
_____
_____
_____
_____
_____
_____
_____
_____
_____
_____
_____
_____
_____

BOOK INFORMATION

BOOK TITLE/SERIES:	
Book # in Series:	Check here if standalone: ☐
Published by:	
Are you paid by a publisher or do you pay a co-author?	
Co-Author Name:	Co-Author Email:
Co-Author Share %:	Frequency of Payments: (Monthly/Quarterly/Annually)
Co-Author Contract Location (Include a copy on the hard drive with the most up-to-date copy of this book including the cover and metadata, like the blurb.):	

Cover Artist:	Email:	Date:
Typography by:	Email:	
Editing by:	Email:	Date:

ISBN:	Format (ebook/audio/paperback/hard cover)	Personal/Amazon/Ingram/Publisher/etc.:
ISBN:	Format (ebook/audio/paperback/hard cover)	Personal/Amazon/Ingram/Publisher/etc.:
ISBN:	Format (ebook/audio/paperback/hard cover)	Personal/Amazon/Ingram/Publisher/etc.:
ISBN:	Format (ebook/audio/paperback/hard cover)	Personal/Amazon/Ingram/Publisher/etc.:
Translation Language:	Translator + Contact:	ISBN + Source:
Translation Language:	Translator + Contact:	ISBN + Source:
Translation Language:	Translator + Contact:	ISBN + Source:

Audiobook Narrator:	Email:	
Amazon ASIN:	B&N ebook:	Apple ebook:
Kobo ebook:	Other:	Other:
Direct Sale Location/Link:		

BOOK INFORMATION

Audiobook Channel:	Date Added:
Audiobook Channel:	Date Added:
Audiobook Channel:	Date Added:
Audiobook Channel:	Date Added:
Audiobook Channel:	Date Added:
Audiobook Channel:	Date Added:

If you have the title optioned for film, put that information here -- who, contact info, and date option ends.

Are there licenses in your digital folders for anything here? These include licenses for cover artwork, distribution, audio, and anything else that requires a license:

ANY OTHER INFORMATION THAT'S UNIQUE TO THIS TITLE/SERIES?

_____
_____
_____
_____
_____
_____
_____
_____
_____
_____
_____
_____
_____
_____

BOOK INFORMATION

BOOK TITLE/SERIES:	
Book # in Series:	Check here if standalone: ☐
Published by:	
Are you paid by a publisher or do you pay a co-author?	
Co-Author Name:	Co-Author Email:
Co-Author Share %:	Frequency of Payments: (Monthly/Quarterly/Annually)
Co-Author Contract Location (Include a copy on the hard drive with the most up-to-date copy of this book including the cover and metadata, like the blurb.):	

Cover Artist:	Email:	Date:
Typography by:	Email:	
Editing by:	Email:	Date:

ISBN:	Format (ebook/audio/paperback/hard cover)	Personal/Amazon/Ingram/Publisher/etc.:
ISBN:	Format (ebook/audio/paperback/hard cover)	Personal/Amazon/Ingram/Publisher/etc.:
ISBN:	Format (ebook/audio/paperback/hard cover)	Personal/Amazon/Ingram/Publisher/etc.:
ISBN:	Format (ebook/audio/paperback/hard cover)	Personal/Amazon/Ingram/Publisher/etc.:
Translation Language:	Translator + Contact:	ISBN + Source:
Translation Language:	Translator + Contact:	ISBN + Source:
Translation Language:	Translator + Contact:	ISBN + Source:

Audiobook Narrator:	Email:	
Amazon ASIN:	B&N ebook:	Apple ebook:
Kobo ebook:	Other:	Other:
Direct Sale Location/Link:		

BOOK INFORMATION

Audiobook Channel:	Date Added:
Audiobook Channel:	Date Added:
Audiobook Channel:	Date Added:
Audiobook Channel:	Date Added:
Audiobook Channel:	Date Added:
Audiobook Channel:	Date Added:

If you have the title optioned for film, put that information here -- who, contact info, and date option ends.

Are there licenses in your digital folders for anything here? These include licenses for cover artwork, distribution, audio, and anything else that requires a license:

ANY OTHER INFORMATION THAT'S UNIQUE TO THIS TITLE/SERIES?

_____
_____
_____
_____
_____
_____
_____
_____
_____
_____
_____
_____

BOOK INFORMATION

BOOK TITLE/SERIES:	
Book # in Series:	Check here if standalone: ☐
Published by:	
Are you paid by a publisher or do you pay a co-author?	
Co-Author Name:	Co-Author Email:
Co-Author Share %:	Frequency of Payments: (Monthly/Quarterly/Annually)
Co-Author Contract Location (Include a copy on the hard drive with the most up-to-date copy of this book including the cover and metadata, like the blurb.):	

Cover Artist:	Email:	Date:
Typography by:	Email:	
Editing by:	Email:	Date:

ISBN:	Format (ebook/audio/paperback/hard cover)	Personal/Amazon/Ingram/Publisher/etc.:
ISBN:	Format (ebook/audio/paperback/hard cover)	Personal/Amazon/Ingram/Publisher/etc.:
ISBN:	Format (ebook/audio/paperback/hard cover)	Personal/Amazon/Ingram/Publisher/etc.:
ISBN:	Format (ebook/audio/paperback/hard cover)	Personal/Amazon/Ingram/Publisher/etc.:
Translation Language:	Translator + Contact:	ISBN + Source:
Translation Language:	Translator + Contact:	ISBN + Source:
Translation Language:	Translator + Contact:	ISBN + Source:

Audiobook Narrator:	Email:	
Amazon ASIN:	B&N ebook:	Apple ebook:
Kobo ebook:	Other:	Other:
Direct Sale Location/Link:		

BOOK INFORMATION

Audiobook Channel:	Date Added:
Audiobook Channel:	Date Added:
Audiobook Channel:	Date Added:
Audiobook Channel:	Date Added:
Audiobook Channel:	Date Added:
Audiobook Channel:	Date Added:

If you have the title optioned for film, put that information here -- who, contact info, and date option ends.

Are there licenses in your digital folders for anything here? These include licenses for cover artwork, distribution, audio, and anything else that requires a license:

ANY OTHER INFORMATION THAT'S UNIQUE TO THIS TITLE/SERIES?

_____
_____
_____
_____
_____
_____
_____
_____
_____
_____
_____
_____
_____

BOOK INFORMATION

BOOK TITLE/SERIES:	
Book # in Series:	Check here if standalone: ☐
Published by:	
Are you paid by a publisher or do you pay a co-author?	
Co-Author Name:	Co-Author Email:
Co-Author Share %:	Frequency of Payments: (Monthly/Quarterly/Annually)
Co-Author Contract Location (Include a copy on the hard drive with the most up-to-date copy of this book including the cover and metadata, like the blurb.):	

Cover Artist:	Email:	Date:
Typography by:	Email:	
Editing by:	Email:	Date:

ISBN:	Format (ebook/audio/paperback/hard cover)	Personal/Amazon/Ingram/Publisher/etc.:
ISBN:	Format (ebook/audio/paperback/hard cover)	Personal/Amazon/Ingram/Publisher/etc.:
ISBN:	Format (ebook/audio/paperback/hard cover)	Personal/Amazon/Ingram/Publisher/etc.:
ISBN:	Format (ebook/audio/paperback/hard cover)	Personal/Amazon/Ingram/Publisher/etc.:
Translation Language:	Translator + Contact:	ISBN + Source:
Translation Language:	Translator + Contact:	ISBN + Source:
Translation Language:	Translator + Contact:	ISBN + Source:

Audiobook Narrator:	Email:	
Amazon ASIN:	B&N ebook:	Apple ebook:
Kobo ebook:	Other:	Other:
Direct Sale Location/Link:		

BOOK INFORMATION

Audiobook Channel:	Date Added:
Audiobook Channel:	Date Added:
Audiobook Channel:	Date Added:
Audiobook Channel:	Date Added:
Audiobook Channel:	Date Added:
Audiobook Channel:	Date Added:
If you have the title optioned for film, put that information here -- who, contact info, and date option ends.	
Are there licenses in your digital folders for anything here? These include licenses for cover artwork, distribution, audio, and anything else that requires a license:	

ANY OTHER INFORMATION THAT'S UNIQUE TO THIS TITLE/SERIES?

BOOK INFORMATION

BOOK TITLE/SERIES:		
Book # in Series:		Check here if standalone: ☐
Published by:		
Are you paid by a publisher or do you pay a co-author?		
Co-Author Name:	Co-Author Email:	
Co-Author Share %:	Frequency of Payments: (Monthly/Quarterly/Annually)	
Co-Author Contract Location (Include a copy on the hard drive with the most up-to-date copy of this book including the cover and metadata, like the blurb.):		
Cover Artist:	Email:	Date:
Typography by:	Email:	
Editing by:	Email:	Date:
ISBN:	Format (ebook/audio/paperback/hard cover)	Personal/Amazon/Ingram/Publisher/etc.:
ISBN:	Format (ebook/audio/paperback/hard cover)	Personal/Amazon/Ingram/Publisher/etc.:
ISBN:	Format (ebook/audio/paperback/hard cover)	Personal/Amazon/Ingram/Publisher/etc.:
ISBN:	Format (ebook/audio/paperback/hard cover)	Personal/Amazon/Ingram/Publisher/etc.:
Translation Language:	Translator + Contact:	ISBN + Source:
Translation Language:	Translator + Contact:	ISBN + Source:
Translation Language:	Translator + Contact:	ISBN + Source:
Audiobook Narrator:	Email:	
Amazon ASIN:	B&N ebook:	Apple ebook:
Kobo ebook:	Other:	Other:
Direct Sale Location/Link:		

BOOK INFORMATION

Audiobook Channel:	Date Added:
Audiobook Channel:	Date Added:
Audiobook Channel:	Date Added:
Audiobook Channel:	Date Added:
Audiobook Channel:	Date Added:
Audiobook Channel:	Date Added:

If you have the title optioned for film, put that information here -- who, contact info, and date option ends.

Are there licenses in your digital folders for anything here? These include licenses for cover artwork, distribution, audio, and anything else that requires a license:

ANY OTHER INFORMATION THAT'S UNIQUE TO THIS TITLE/SERIES?

_____
_____
_____
_____
_____
_____
_____
_____
_____
_____
_____
_____
_____

BOOK INFORMATION

BOOK TITLE/SERIES:	
Book # in Series:	Check here if standalone: ☐
Published by:	
Are you paid by a publisher or do you pay a co-author?	
Co-Author Name:	Co-Author Email:
Co-Author Share %:	Frequency of Payments: (Monthly/Quarterly/Annually)
Co-Author Contract Location (Include a copy on the hard drive with the most up-to-date copy of this book including the cover and metadata, like the blurb.):	

Cover Artist:	Email:	Date:
Typography by:	Email:	
Editing by:	Email:	Date:

ISBN:	Format (ebook/audio/paperback/hard cover)	Personal/Amazon/Ingram/Publisher/etc.:
ISBN:	Format (ebook/audio/paperback/hard cover)	Personal/Amazon/Ingram/Publisher/etc.:
ISBN:	Format (ebook/audio/paperback/hard cover)	Personal/Amazon/Ingram/Publisher/etc.:
ISBN:	Format (ebook/audio/paperback/hard cover)	Personal/Amazon/Ingram/Publisher/etc.:
Translation Language:	Translator + Contact:	ISBN + Source:
Translation Language:	Translator + Contact:	ISBN + Source:
Translation Language:	Translator + Contact:	ISBN + Source:

Audiobook Narrator:	Email:	
Amazon ASIN:	B&N ebook:	Apple ebook:
Kobo ebook:	Other:	Other:
Direct Sale Location/Link:		

BOOK INFORMATION

Audiobook Channel:	Date Added:
Audiobook Channel:	Date Added:
Audiobook Channel:	Date Added:
Audiobook Channel:	Date Added:
Audiobook Channel:	Date Added:
Audiobook Channel:	Date Added:

If you have the title optioned for film, put that information here -- who, contact info, and date option ends.

Are there licenses in your digital folders for anything here? These include licenses for cover artwork, distribution, audio, and anything else that requires a license:

ANY OTHER INFORMATION THAT'S UNIQUE TO THIS TITLE/SERIES?

_____
_____
_____
_____
_____
_____
_____
_____
_____
_____
_____
_____
_____
_____

BOOK INFORMATION

BOOK TITLE/SERIES:	
Book # in Series:	Check here if standalone: ☐
Published by:	
Are you paid by a publisher or do you pay a co-author?	
Co-Author Name:	Co-Author Email:
Co-Author Share %:	Frequency of Payments: (Monthly/Quarterly/Annually)
Co-Author Contract Location (Include a copy on the hard drive with the most up-to-date copy of this book including the cover and metadata, like the blurb.):	

Cover Artist:	Email:	Date:
Typography by:	Email:	
Editing by:	Email:	Date:

ISBN:	Format (ebook/audio/paperback/hard cover)	Personal/Amazon/Ingram/Publisher/etc.:
ISBN:	Format (ebook/audio/paperback/hard cover)	Personal/Amazon/Ingram/Publisher/etc.:
ISBN:	Format (ebook/audio/paperback/hard cover)	Personal/Amazon/Ingram/Publisher/etc.:
ISBN:	Format (ebook/audio/paperback/hard cover)	Personal/Amazon/Ingram/Publisher/etc.:

Translation Language:	Translator + Contact:	ISBN + Source:
Translation Language:	Translator + Contact:	ISBN + Source:
Translation Language:	Translator + Contact:	ISBN + Source:

Audiobook Narrator:	Email:	
Amazon ASIN:	B&N ebook:	Apple ebook:
Kobo ebook:	Other:	Other:
Direct Sale Location/Link:		

BOOK INFORMATION

Audiobook Channel:	Date Added:
Audiobook Channel:	Date Added:
Audiobook Channel:	Date Added:
Audiobook Channel:	Date Added:
Audiobook Channel:	Date Added:
Audiobook Channel:	Date Added:

If you have the title optioned for film, put that information here -- who, contact info, and date option ends.

Are there licenses in your digital folders for anything here? These include licenses for cover artwork, distribution, audio, and anything else that requires a license:

ANY OTHER INFORMATION THAT'S UNIQUE TO THIS TITLE/SERIES?

_____
_____
_____
_____
_____
_____
_____
_____
_____
_____
_____
_____
_____
_____

BOOK INFORMATION

BOOK TITLE/SERIES:	
Book # in Series:	Check here if standalone: ☐
Published by:	
Are you paid by a publisher or do you pay a co-author?	

Co-Author Name:	Co-Author Email:
Co-Author Share %:	Frequency of Payments: (Monthly/Quarterly/Annually)

Co-Author Contract Location (Include a copy on the hard drive with the most up-to-date copy of this book including the cover and metadata, like the blurb.):

Cover Artist:	Email:	Date:
Typography by:	Email:	
Editing by:	Email:	Date:

ISBN:	Format (ebook/audio/paperback/hard cover)	Personal/Amazon/Ingram/Publisher/etc.:
ISBN:	Format (ebook/audio/paperback/hard cover)	Personal/Amazon/Ingram/Publisher/etc.:
ISBN:	Format (ebook/audio/paperback/hard cover)	Personal/Amazon/Ingram/Publisher/etc.:
ISBN:	Format (ebook/audio/paperback/hard cover)	Personal/Amazon/Ingram/Publisher/etc.:

Translation Language:	Translator + Contact:	ISBN + Source:
Translation Language:	Translator + Contact:	ISBN + Source:
Translation Language:	Translator + Contact:	ISBN + Source:

Audiobook Narrator:	Email:	
Amazon ASIN:	B&N ebook:	Apple ebook:
Kobo ebook:	Other:	Other:
Direct Sale Location/Link:		

BOOK INFORMATION

Audiobook Channel:	Date Added:
Audiobook Channel:	Date Added:
Audiobook Channel:	Date Added:
Audiobook Channel:	Date Added:
Audiobook Channel:	Date Added:
Audiobook Channel:	Date Added:

If you have the title optioned for film, put that information here -- who, contact info, and date option ends.

Are there licenses in your digital folders for anything here? These include licenses for cover artwork, distribution, audio, and anything else that requires a license:

ANY OTHER INFORMATION THAT'S UNIQUE TO THIS TITLE/SERIES?

BOOK INFORMATION

BOOK TITLE/SERIES:	
Book # in Series:	Check here if standalone: ☐
Published by:	
Are you paid by a publisher or do you pay a co-author?	
Co-Author Name:	Co-Author Email:
Co-Author Share %:	Frequency of Payments: (Monthly/Quarterly/Annually)
Co-Author Contract Location (Include a copy on the hard drive with the most up-to-date copy of this book including the cover and metadata, like the blurb.):	

Cover Artist:	Email:	Date:
Typography by:	Email:	
Editing by:	Email:	Date:

ISBN:	Format (ebook/audio/paperback/hard cover)	Personal/Amazon/Ingram/Publisher/etc.:
ISBN:	Format (ebook/audio/paperback/hard cover)	Personal/Amazon/Ingram/Publisher/etc.:
ISBN:	Format (ebook/audio/paperback/hard cover)	Personal/Amazon/Ingram/Publisher/etc.:
ISBN:	Format (ebook/audio/paperback/hard cover)	Personal/Amazon/Ingram/Publisher/etc.:
Translation Language:	Translator + Contact:	ISBN + Source:
Translation Language:	Translator + Contact:	ISBN + Source:
Translation Language:	Translator + Contact:	ISBN + Source:

Audiobook Narrator:	Email:	
Amazon ASIN:	B&N ebook:	Apple ebook:
Kobo ebook:	Other:	Other:
Direct Sale Location/Link:		

BOOK INFORMATION

Audiobook Channel:	Date Added:
Audiobook Channel:	Date Added:
Audiobook Channel:	Date Added:
Audiobook Channel:	Date Added:
Audiobook Channel:	Date Added:
Audiobook Channel:	Date Added:

If you have the title optioned for film, put that information here -- who, contact info, and date option ends.

Are there licenses in your digital folders for anything here? These include licenses for cover artwork, distribution, audio, and anything else that requires a license:

ANY OTHER INFORMATION THAT'S UNIQUE TO THIS TITLE/SERIES?

_____
_____
_____
_____
_____
_____
_____
_____
_____
_____
_____
_____
_____

BOOK INFORMATION

BOOK TITLE/SERIES:	
Book # in Series:	Check here if standalone: ☐
Published by:	
Are you paid by a publisher or do you pay a co-author?	
Co-Author Name:	Co-Author Email:
Co-Author Share %:	Frequency of Payments: (Monthly/Quarterly/Annually)
Co-Author Contract Location (Include a copy on the hard drive with the most up-to-date copy of this book including the cover and metadata, like the blurb.):	

Cover Artist:	Email:	Date:
Typography by:	Email:	
Editing by:	Email:	Date:

ISBN:	Format (ebook/audio/paperback/hard cover)	Personal/Amazon/Ingram/Publisher/etc.:
ISBN:	Format (ebook/audio/paperback/hard cover)	Personal/Amazon/Ingram/Publisher/etc.:
ISBN:	Format (ebook/audio/paperback/hard cover)	Personal/Amazon/Ingram/Publisher/etc.:
ISBN:	Format (ebook/audio/paperback/hard cover)	Personal/Amazon/Ingram/Publisher/etc.:
Translation Language:	Translator + Contact:	ISBN + Source:
Translation Language:	Translator + Contact:	ISBN + Source:
Translation Language:	Translator + Contact:	ISBN + Source:

Audiobook Narrator:	Email:	
Amazon ASIN:	B&N ebook:	Apple ebook:
Kobo ebook:	Other:	Other:
Direct Sale Location/Link:		

BOOK INFORMATION

Audiobook Channel:	Date Added:
Audiobook Channel:	Date Added:
Audiobook Channel:	Date Added:
Audiobook Channel:	Date Added:
Audiobook Channel:	Date Added:
Audiobook Channel:	Date Added:

If you have the title optioned for film, put that information here -- who, contact info, and date option ends.

Are there licenses in your digital folders for anything here? These include licenses for cover artwork, distribution, audio, and anything else that requires a license:

ANY OTHER INFORMATION THAT'S UNIQUE TO THIS TITLE/SERIES?

_____
_____
_____
_____
_____
_____
_____
_____
_____
_____
_____
_____
_____
_____

BOOK INFORMATION

BOOK TITLE/SERIES:

Book # in Series: | Check here if standalone: ☐

Published by:

Are you paid by a publisher or do you pay a co-author?

Co-Author Name:	Co-Author Email:
Co-Author Share %:	Frequency of Payments: (Monthly/Quarterly/Annually)

Co-Author Contract Location (Include a copy on the hard drive with the most up-to-date copy of this book including the cover and metadata, like the blurb.):

Cover Artist:	Email:	Date:
Typography by:	Email:	
Editing by:	Email:	Date:
ISBN:	Format (ebook/audio/paperback/hard cover)	Personal/Amazon/Ingram/Publisher/etc.:
ISBN:	Format (ebook/audio/paperback/hard cover)	Personal/Amazon/Ingram/Publisher/etc.:
ISBN:	Format (ebook/audio/paperback/hard cover)	Personal/Amazon/Ingram/Publisher/etc.:
ISBN:	Format (ebook/audio/paperback/hard cover)	Personal/Amazon/Ingram/Publisher/etc.:
Translation Language:	Translator + Contact:	ISBN + Source:
Translation Language:	Translator + Contact:	ISBN + Source:
Translation Language:	Translator + Contact:	ISBN + Source:

Audiobook Narrator:	Email:	
Amazon ASIN:	B&N ebook:	Apple ebook:
Kobo ebook:	Other:	Other:

Direct Sale Location/Link:

BOOK INFORMATION

Audiobook Channel:	Date Added:
Audiobook Channel:	Date Added:
Audiobook Channel:	Date Added:
Audiobook Channel:	Date Added:
Audiobook Channel:	Date Added:
Audiobook Channel:	Date Added:

If you have the title optioned for film, put that information here -- who, contact info, and date option ends.

Are there licenses in your digital folders for anything here? These include licenses for cover artwork, distribution, audio, and anything else that requires a license:

ANY OTHER INFORMATION THAT'S UNIQUE TO THIS TITLE/SERIES?

_____
_____
_____
_____
_____
_____
_____
_____
_____
_____
_____
_____

BOOK INFORMATION

BOOK TITLE/SERIES:	
Book # in Series:	Check here if standalone: ☐
Published by:	
Are you paid by a publisher or do you pay a co-author?	
Co-Author Name:	Co-Author Email:
Co-Author Share %:	Frequency of Payments: (Monthly/Quarterly/Annually)
Co-Author Contract Location (Include a copy on the hard drive with the most up-to-date copy of this book including the cover and metadata, like the blurb.):	

Cover Artist:	Email:	Date:
Typography by:	Email:	
Editing by:	Email:	Date:

ISBN:	Format (ebook/audio/paperback/hard cover)	Personal/Amazon/Ingram/Publisher/etc.:
ISBN:	Format (ebook/audio/paperback/hard cover)	Personal/Amazon/Ingram/Publisher/etc.:
ISBN:	Format (ebook/audio/paperback/hard cover)	Personal/Amazon/Ingram/Publisher/etc.:
ISBN:	Format (ebook/audio/paperback/hard cover)	Personal/Amazon/Ingram/Publisher/etc.:
Translation Language:	Translator + Contact:	ISBN + Source:
Translation Language:	Translator + Contact:	ISBN + Source:
Translation Language:	Translator + Contact:	ISBN + Source:

Audiobook Narrator:	Email:	
Amazon ASIN:	B&N ebook:	Apple ebook:
Kobo ebook:	Other:	Other:
Direct Sale Location/Link:		

BOOK INFORMATION

Audiobook Channel:	Date Added:
Audiobook Channel:	Date Added:
Audiobook Channel:	Date Added:
Audiobook Channel:	Date Added:
Audiobook Channel:	Date Added:
Audiobook Channel:	Date Added:

If you have the title optioned for film, put that information here -- who, contact info, and date option ends.

Are there licenses in your digital folders for anything here? These include licenses for cover artwork, distribution, audio, and anything else that requires a license:

ANY OTHER INFORMATION THAT'S UNIQUE TO THIS TITLE/SERIES?

___
___
___
___
___
___
___
___
___
___
___
___
___
___

BOOK INFORMATION

BOOK TITLE/SERIES:	
Book # in Series:	Check here if standalone: ☐
Published by:	
Are you paid by a publisher or do you pay a co-author?	
Co-Author Name:	Co-Author Email:
Co-Author Share %:	Frequency of Payments: (Monthly/Quarterly/Annually)
Co-Author Contract Location (Include a copy on the hard drive with the most up-to-date copy of this book including the cover and metadata, like the blurb.):	

Cover Artist:	Email:	Date:
Typography by:	Email:	
Editing by:	Email:	Date:

ISBN:	Format (ebook/audio/paperback/hard cover)	Personal/Amazon/Ingram/Publisher/etc.:
ISBN:	Format (ebook/audio/paperback/hard cover)	Personal/Amazon/Ingram/Publisher/etc.:
ISBN:	Format (ebook/audio/paperback/hard cover)	Personal/Amazon/Ingram/Publisher/etc.:
ISBN:	Format (ebook/audio/paperback/hard cover)	Personal/Amazon/Ingram/Publisher/etc.:
Translation Language:	Translator + Contact:	ISBN + Source:
Translation Language:	Translator + Contact:	ISBN + Source:
Translation Language:	Translator + Contact:	ISBN + Source:

Audiobook Narrator:	Email:	
Amazon ASIN:	B&N ebook:	Apple ebook:
Kobo ebook:	Other:	Other:
Direct Sale Location/Link:		

BOOK INFORMATION

Audiobook Channel:	Date Added:
Audiobook Channel:	Date Added:
Audiobook Channel:	Date Added:
Audiobook Channel:	Date Added:
Audiobook Channel:	Date Added:
Audiobook Channel:	Date Added:

If you have the title optioned for film, put that information here -- who, contact info, and date option ends.

Are there licenses in your digital folders for anything here? These include licenses for cover artwork, distribution, audio, and anything else that requires a license:

ANY OTHER INFORMATION THAT'S UNIQUE TO THIS TITLE/SERIES?

_____
_____
_____
_____
_____
_____
_____
_____
_____
_____
_____
_____
_____
_____

BOOK INFORMATION

BOOK TITLE/SERIES:	
Book # in Series:	Check here if standalone: ☐
Published by:	
Are you paid by a publisher or do you pay a co-author?	
Co-Author Name:	Co-Author Email:
Co-Author Share %:	Frequency of Payments: (Monthly/Quarterly/Annually)
Co-Author Contract Location (Include a copy on the hard drive with the most up-to-date copy of this book including the cover and metadata, like the blurb.):	

Cover Artist:	Email:	Date:
Typography by:	Email:	
Editing by:	Email:	Date:

ISBN:	Format (ebook/audio/paperback/hard cover)	Personal/Amazon/Ingram/Publisher/etc.:
ISBN:	Format (ebook/audio/paperback/hard cover)	Personal/Amazon/Ingram/Publisher/etc.:
ISBN:	Format (ebook/audio/paperback/hard cover)	Personal/Amazon/Ingram/Publisher/etc.:
ISBN:	Format (ebook/audio/paperback/hard cover)	Personal/Amazon/Ingram/Publisher/etc.:

Translation Language:	Translator + Contact:	ISBN + Source:
Translation Language:	Translator + Contact:	ISBN + Source:
Translation Language:	Translator + Contact:	ISBN + Source:

Audiobook Narrator:	Email:	
Amazon ASIN:	B&N ebook:	Apple ebook:
Kobo ebook:	Other:	Other:
Direct Sale Location/Link:		

BOOK INFORMATION

Audiobook Channel:	Date Added:
Audiobook Channel:	Date Added:
Audiobook Channel:	Date Added:
Audiobook Channel:	Date Added:
Audiobook Channel:	Date Added:
Audiobook Channel:	Date Added:

If you have the title optioned for film, put that information here -- who, contact info, and date option ends.

Are there licenses in your digital folders for anything here? These include licenses for cover artwork, distribution, audio, and anything else that requires a license:

ANY OTHER INFORMATION THAT'S UNIQUE TO THIS TITLE/SERIES?

_____
_____
_____
_____
_____
_____
_____
_____
_____
_____
_____
_____
_____
_____

BOOK INFORMATION

BOOK TITLE/SERIES:		
Book # in Series:		Check here if standalone: ☐
Published by:		
Are you paid by a publisher or do you pay a co-author?		
Co-Author Name:	Co-Author Email:	
Co-Author Share %:	Frequency of Payments: (Monthly/Quarterly/Annually)	
Co-Author Contract Location (Include a copy on the hard drive with the most up-to-date copy of this book including the cover and metadata, like the blurb.):		
Cover Artist:	Email:	Date:
Typography by:	Email:	
Editing by:	Email:	Date:
ISBN:	Format (ebook/audio/paperback/hard cover)	Personal/Amazon/Ingram/Publisher/etc.:
ISBN:	Format (ebook/audio/paperback/hard cover)	Personal/Amazon/Ingram/Publisher/etc.:
ISBN:	Format (ebook/audio/paperback/hard cover)	Personal/Amazon/Ingram/Publisher/etc.:
ISBN:	Format (ebook/audio/paperback/hard cover)	Personal/Amazon/Ingram/Publisher/etc.:
Translation Language:	Translator + Contact:	ISBN + Source:
Translation Language:	Translator + Contact:	ISBN + Source:
Translation Language:	Translator + Contact:	ISBN + Source:
Audiobook Narrator:	Email:	
Amazon ASIN:	B&N ebook:	Apple ebook:
Kobo ebook:	Other:	Other:
Direct Sale Location/Link:		

BOOK INFORMATION

Audiobook Channel:	Date Added:
Audiobook Channel:	Date Added:
Audiobook Channel:	Date Added:
Audiobook Channel:	Date Added:
Audiobook Channel:	Date Added:
Audiobook Channel:	Date Added:
If you have the title optioned for film, put that information here -- who, contact info, and date option ends.	
Are there licenses in your digital folders for anything here? These include licenses for cover artwork, distribution, audio, and anything else that requires a license:	

ANY OTHER INFORMATION THAT'S UNIQUE TO THIS TITLE/SERIES?

_____
_____
_____
_____
_____
_____
_____
_____
_____
_____
_____
_____
_____
_____

BOOK INFORMATION

BOOK TITLE/SERIES:		
Book # in Series:		Check here if standalone: ☐
Published by:		
Are you paid by a publisher or do you pay a co-author?		
Co-Author Name:	Co-Author Email:	
Co-Author Share %:	Frequency of Payments: (Monthly/Quarterly/Annually)	
Co-Author Contract Location (Include a copy on the hard drive with the most up-to-date copy of this book including the cover and metadata, like the blurb.):		
Cover Artist:	Email:	Date:
Typography by:	Email:	
Editing by:	Email:	Date:
ISBN:	Format (ebook/audio/paperback/hard cover)	Personal/Amazon/Ingram/Publisher/etc.:
ISBN:	Format (ebook/audio/paperback/hard cover)	Personal/Amazon/Ingram/Publisher/etc.:
ISBN:	Format (ebook/audio/paperback/hard cover)	Personal/Amazon/Ingram/Publisher/etc.:
ISBN:	Format (ebook/audio/paperback/hard cover)	Personal/Amazon/Ingram/Publisher/etc.:
Translation Language:	Translator + Contact:	ISBN + Source:
Translation Language:	Translator + Contact:	ISBN + Source:
Translation Language:	Translator + Contact:	ISBN + Source:
Audiobook Narrator:	Email:	
Amazon ASIN:	B&N ebook:	Apple ebook:
Kobo ebook:	Other:	Other:
Direct Sale Location/Link:		

BOOK INFORMATION

Audiobook Channel:	Date Added:
Audiobook Channel:	Date Added:
Audiobook Channel:	Date Added:
Audiobook Channel:	Date Added:
Audiobook Channel:	Date Added:
Audiobook Channel:	Date Added:

If you have the title optioned for film, put that information here -- who, contact info, and date option ends.

Are there licenses in your digital folders for anything here? These include licenses for cover artwork, distribution, audio, and anything else that requires a license:

ANY OTHER INFORMATION THAT'S UNIQUE TO THIS TITLE/SERIES?

_____
_____
_____
_____
_____
_____
_____
_____
_____
_____
_____
_____
_____

BOOK INFORMATION

BOOK TITLE/SERIES:	
Book # in Series:	Check here if standalone: ☐
Published by:	
Are you paid by a publisher or do you pay a co-author?	
Co-Author Name:	Co-Author Email:
Co-Author Share %:	Frequency of Payments: (Monthly/Quarterly/Annually)
Co-Author Contract Location (Include a copy on the hard drive with the most up-to-date copy of this book including the cover and metadata, like the blurb.):	
Cover Artist:	Email:	Date:
Typography by:	Email:
Editing by:	Email:	Date:
ISBN:	Format (ebook/audio/paperback/hard cover)	Personal/Amazon/Ingram/Publisher/etc.:
ISBN:	Format (ebook/audio/paperback/hard cover)	Personal/Amazon/Ingram/Publisher/etc.:
ISBN:	Format (ebook/audio/paperback/hard cover)	Personal/Amazon/Ingram/Publisher/etc.:
ISBN:	Format (ebook/audio/paperback/hard cover)	Personal/Amazon/Ingram/Publisher/etc.:
Translation Language:	Translator + Contact:	ISBN + Source:
Translation Language:	Translator + Contact:	ISBN + Source:
Translation Language:	Translator + Contact:	ISBN + Source:
Audiobook Narrator:	Email:
Amazon ASIN:	B&N ebook:	Apple ebook:
Kobo ebook:	Other:	Other:
Direct Sale Location/Link:	

BOOK INFORMATION

Audiobook Channel:	Date Added:
Audiobook Channel:	Date Added:
Audiobook Channel:	Date Added:
Audiobook Channel:	Date Added:
Audiobook Channel:	Date Added:
Audiobook Channel:	Date Added:

If you have the title optioned for film, put that information here -- who, contact info, and date option ends.

Are there licenses in your digital folders for anything here? These include licenses for cover artwork, distribution, audio, and anything else that requires a license:

ANY OTHER INFORMATION THAT'S UNIQUE TO THIS TITLE/SERIES?

_____
_____
_____
_____
_____
_____
_____
_____
_____
_____
_____
_____
_____

BOOK INFORMATION

BOOK TITLE/SERIES:	
Book # in Series:	Check here if standalone: ☐
Published by:	
Are you paid by a publisher or do you pay a co-author?	
Co-Author Name:	Co-Author Email:
Co-Author Share %:	Frequency of Payments: (Monthly/Quarterly/Annually)
Co-Author Contract Location (Include a copy on the hard drive with the most up-to-date copy of this book including the cover and metadata, like the blurb.):	

Cover Artist:	Email:	Date:
Typography by:	Email:	
Editing by:	Email:	Date:

ISBN:	Format (ebook/audio/paperback/hard cover)	Personal/Amazon/Ingram/Publisher/etc.:
ISBN:	Format (ebook/audio/paperback/hard cover)	Personal/Amazon/Ingram/Publisher/etc.:
ISBN:	Format (ebook/audio/paperback/hard cover)	Personal/Amazon/Ingram/Publisher/etc.:
ISBN:	Format (ebook/audio/paperback/hard cover)	Personal/Amazon/Ingram/Publisher/etc.:
Translation Language:	Translator + Contact:	ISBN + Source:
Translation Language:	Translator + Contact:	ISBN + Source:
Translation Language:	Translator + Contact:	ISBN + Source:

Audiobook Narrator:	Email:	
Amazon ASIN:	B&N ebook:	Apple ebook:
Kobo ebook:	Other:	Other:
Direct Sale Location/Link:		

BOOK INFORMATION

Audiobook Channel:	Date Added:
Audiobook Channel:	Date Added:
Audiobook Channel:	Date Added:
Audiobook Channel:	Date Added:
Audiobook Channel:	Date Added:
Audiobook Channel:	Date Added:
If you have the title optioned for film, put that information here -- who, contact info, and date option ends.	
Are there licenses in your digital folders for anything here? These include licenses for cover artwork, distribution, audio, and anything else that requires a license:	

ANY OTHER INFORMATION THAT'S UNIQUE TO THIS TITLE/SERIES?

_____
_____
_____
_____
_____
_____
_____
_____
_____
_____
_____
_____
_____

BOOK INFORMATION

BOOK TITLE/SERIES:	
Book # in Series:	Check here if standalone: ☐
Published by:	
Are you paid by a publisher or do you pay a co-author?	
Co-Author Name:	Co-Author Email:
Co-Author Share %:	Frequency of Payments: (Monthly/Quarterly/Annually)
Co-Author Contract Location (Include a copy on the hard drive with the most up-to-date copy of this book including the cover and metadata, like the blurb.):	

Cover Artist:	Email:	Date:
Typography by:	Email:	
Editing by:	Email:	Date:

ISBN:	Format (ebook/audio/paperback/hard cover)	Personal/Amazon/Ingram/Publisher/etc.:
ISBN:	Format (ebook/audio/paperback/hard cover)	Personal/Amazon/Ingram/Publisher/etc.:
ISBN:	Format (ebook/audio/paperback/hard cover)	Personal/Amazon/Ingram/Publisher/etc.:
ISBN:	Format (ebook/audio/paperback/hard cover)	Personal/Amazon/Ingram/Publisher/etc.:
Translation Language:	Translator + Contact:	ISBN + Source:
Translation Language:	Translator + Contact:	ISBN + Source:
Translation Language:	Translator + Contact:	ISBN + Source:

Audiobook Narrator:	Email:	
Amazon ASIN:	B&N ebook:	Apple ebook:
Kobo ebook:	Other:	Other:
Direct Sale Location/Link:		

BOOK INFORMATION

Audiobook Channel:	Date Added:
Audiobook Channel:	Date Added:
Audiobook Channel:	Date Added:
Audiobook Channel:	Date Added:
Audiobook Channel:	Date Added:
Audiobook Channel:	Date Added:

If you have the title optioned for film, put that information here -- who, contact info, and date option ends.

Are there licenses in your digital folders for anything here? These include licenses for cover artwork, distribution, audio, and anything else that requires a license:

ANY OTHER INFORMATION THAT'S UNIQUE TO THIS TITLE/SERIES?

_____
_____
_____
_____
_____
_____
_____
_____
_____
_____
_____
_____

BOOK INFORMATION

BOOK TITLE/SERIES:	
Book # in Series:	Check here if standalone: ☐
Published by:	
Are you paid by a publisher or do you pay a co-author?	
Co-Author Name:	Co-Author Email:
Co-Author Share %:	Frequency of Payments: (Monthly/Quarterly/Annually)
Co-Author Contract Location (Include a copy on the hard drive with the most up-to-date copy of this book including the cover and metadata, like the blurb.):	

Cover Artist:	Email:	Date:
Typography by:	Email:	
Editing by:	Email:	Date:

ISBN:	Format (ebook/audio/paperback/hard cover)	Personal/Amazon/Ingram/Publisher/etc.:
ISBN:	Format (ebook/audio/paperback/hard cover)	Personal/Amazon/Ingram/Publisher/etc.:
ISBN:	Format (ebook/audio/paperback/hard cover)	Personal/Amazon/Ingram/Publisher/etc.:
ISBN:	Format (ebook/audio/paperback/hard cover)	Personal/Amazon/Ingram/Publisher/etc.:
Translation Language:	Translator + Contact:	ISBN + Source:
Translation Language:	Translator + Contact:	ISBN + Source:
Translation Language:	Translator + Contact:	ISBN + Source:

Audiobook Narrator:	Email:	
Amazon ASIN:	B&N ebook:	Apple ebook:
Kobo ebook:	Other:	Other:
Direct Sale Location/Link:		

BOOK INFORMATION

Audiobook Channel:	Date Added:
Audiobook Channel:	Date Added:
Audiobook Channel:	Date Added:
Audiobook Channel:	Date Added:
Audiobook Channel:	Date Added:
Audiobook Channel:	Date Added:

If you have the title optioned for film, put that information here -- who, contact info, and date option ends.

Are there licenses in your digital folders for anything here? These include licenses for cover artwork, distribution, audio, and anything else that requires a license:

ANY OTHER INFORMATION THAT'S UNIQUE TO THIS TITLE/SERIES?

_____
_____
_____
_____
_____
_____
_____
_____
_____
_____
_____
_____
_____

BOOK INFORMATION

BOOK TITLE/SERIES:			
Book # in Series:		Check here if standalone: ☐	
Published by:			
Are you paid by a publisher or do you pay a co-author?			
Co-Author Name:		Co-Author Email:	
Co-Author Share %:		Frequency of Payments: (Monthly/Quarterly/Annually)	
Co-Author Contract Location (Include a copy on the hard drive with the most up-to-date copy of this book including the cover and metadata, like the blurb.):			
Cover Artist:		Email:	Date:
Typography by:		Email:	
Editing by:		Email:	Date:
ISBN:	Format (ebook/audio/paperback/hard cover)		Personal/Amazon/Ingram/Publisher/etc.:
ISBN:	Format (ebook/audio/paperback/hard cover)		Personal/Amazon/Ingram/Publisher/etc.:
ISBN:	Format (ebook/audio/paperback/hard cover)		Personal/Amazon/Ingram/Publisher/etc.:
ISBN:	Format (ebook/audio/paperback/hard cover)		Personal/Amazon/Ingram/Publisher/etc.:
Translation Language:	Translator + Contact:		ISBN + Source:
Translation Language:	Translator + Contact:		ISBN + Source:
Translation Language:	Translator + Contact:		ISBN + Source:
Audiobook Narrator:		Email:	
Amazon ASIN:	B&N ebook:		Apple ebook:
Kobo ebook:	Other:		Other:
Direct Sale Location/Link:			

BOOK INFORMATION

Audiobook Channel:	Date Added:
Audiobook Channel:	Date Added:
Audiobook Channel:	Date Added:
Audiobook Channel:	Date Added:
Audiobook Channel:	Date Added:
Audiobook Channel:	Date Added:
If you have the title optioned for film, put that information here -- who, contact info, and date option ends.	
Are there licenses in your digital folders for anything here? These include licenses for cover artwork, distribution, audio, and anything else that requires a license:	

ANY OTHER INFORMATION THAT'S UNIQUE TO THIS TITLE/SERIES?

_____
_____
_____
_____
_____
_____
_____
_____
_____
_____
_____
_____
_____
_____

BOOK INFORMATION

BOOK TITLE/SERIES:		
Book # in Series:		Check here if standalone: ☐
Published by:		
Are you paid by a publisher or do you pay a co-author?		
Co-Author Name:		Co-Author Email:
Co-Author Share %:		Frequency of Payments: (Monthly/Quarterly/Annually)
Co-Author Contract Location (Include a copy on the hard drive with the most up-to-date copy of this book including the cover and metadata, like the blurb.):		
Cover Artist:	Email:	Date:
Typography by:	Email:	
Editing by:	Email:	Date:
ISBN:	Format (ebook/audio/paperback/hard cover)	Personal/Amazon/Ingram/Publisher/etc.:
ISBN:	Format (ebook/audio/paperback/hard cover)	Personal/Amazon/Ingram/Publisher/etc.:
ISBN:	Format (ebook/audio/paperback/hard cover)	Personal/Amazon/Ingram/Publisher/etc.:
ISBN:	Format (ebook/audio/paperback/hard cover)	Personal/Amazon/Ingram/Publisher/etc.:
Translation Language:	Translator + Contact:	ISBN + Source:
Translation Language:	Translator + Contact:	ISBN + Source:
Translation Language:	Translator + Contact:	ISBN + Source:
Audiobook Narrator:	Email:	
Amazon ASIN:	B&N ebook:	Apple ebook:
Kobo ebook:	Other:	Other:
Direct Sale Location/Link:		

BOOK INFORMATION

Audiobook Channel:	Date Added:
Audiobook Channel:	Date Added:
Audiobook Channel:	Date Added:
Audiobook Channel:	Date Added:
Audiobook Channel:	Date Added:
Audiobook Channel:	Date Added:

If you have the title optioned for film, put that information here -- who, contact info, and date option ends.

Are there licenses in your digital folders for anything here? These include licenses for cover artwork, distribution, audio, and anything else that requires a license:

ANY OTHER INFORMATION THAT'S UNIQUE TO THIS TITLE/SERIES?

BOOK INFORMATION

BOOK TITLE/SERIES:	
Book # in Series:	Check here if standalone: ☐
Published by:	
Are you paid by a publisher or do you pay a co-author?	
Co-Author Name:	Co-Author Email:
Co-Author Share %:	Frequency of Payments: (Monthly/Quarterly/Annually)
Co-Author Contract Location (Include a copy on the hard drive with the most up-to-date copy of this book including the cover and metadata, like the blurb.):	

Cover Artist:	Email:	Date:
Typography by:	Email:	
Editing by:	Email:	Date:

ISBN:	Format (ebook/audio/paperback/hard cover)	Personal/Amazon/Ingram/Publisher/etc.:
ISBN:	Format (ebook/audio/paperback/hard cover)	Personal/Amazon/Ingram/Publisher/etc.:
ISBN:	Format (ebook/audio/paperback/hard cover)	Personal/Amazon/Ingram/Publisher/etc.:
ISBN:	Format (ebook/audio/paperback/hard cover)	Personal/Amazon/Ingram/Publisher/etc.:
Translation Language:	Translator + Contact:	ISBN + Source:
Translation Language:	Translator + Contact:	ISBN + Source:
Translation Language:	Translator + Contact:	ISBN + Source:

Audiobook Narrator:	Email:	
Amazon ASIN:	B&N ebook:	Apple ebook:
Kobo ebook:	Other:	Other:
Direct Sale Location/Link:		

BOOK INFORMATION

Audiobook Channel:	Date Added:
Audiobook Channel:	Date Added:
Audiobook Channel:	Date Added:
Audiobook Channel:	Date Added:
Audiobook Channel:	Date Added:
Audiobook Channel:	Date Added:

If you have the title optioned for film, put that information here -- who, contact info, and date option ends.

Are there licenses in your digital folders for anything here? These include licenses for cover artwork, distribution, audio, and anything else that requires a license:

ANY OTHER INFORMATION THAT'S UNIQUE TO THIS TITLE/SERIES?

_____
_____
_____
_____
_____
_____
_____
_____
_____
_____
_____
_____

BOOK INFORMATION

Any final notes regarding your books.

AUTHOR ACCOUNTS

AUTHOR ACCOUNTS

Put your keys to the castle here and then keep this planner in a lockbox. All of this information is also in the spreadsheet you can download from Google Sheets. It will probably be easier to copy/paste links and then print the pages to insert here.

That being said, your distributors will each require something a little bit different. Amazon has said that they'll close the deceased author's account the second Amazon is notified of the author's passing. That is not optimal. It's critical that others have access to your account—and two-factor authentication—so the IP can be incrementally moved to an account that the estate controls. Other distributors may not delete the account, but they could require a probate order designating who is authorized to access it.

Spreadsheet – An Author's Legacy - https://geni.us/AnAuthorsLegacy

You'll have to download the file to the type of your choice, like Google Sheets or Excel. This file can only be viewed via Google. Also, please do not share this spreadsheet – it is exclusively for the use of those who bought this planner.

YOUR EQUIPMENT / PHYSICAL TOOLS		
Primary Computer Login:	Password:	As of Date:
2nd Computer Login:	Password:	As of Date:
3rd Computer Login:	Password:	As of Date:
Tablet Login:	Password:	As of Date:
Smart Phone Login:	Password:	As of Date:
Physical Storage Device:	Password:	As of Date:
Physical Storage Device:	Password:	As of Date:
Physical Storage Device:	Password:	As of Date:
Physical Storage Device:	Password:	As of Date:
What software do you need to read your book files (Word/Pages/Scrivener/Atticus/etc.):		

AUTHOR ACCOUNTS

WEBSITES & DIGITAL STOREFRONTS

Primary Website Domain Name:	Purchased from:	Login:	Password:	Maintained by:
Other Website Logins (cpanel, etc.):	Purchased from:	Login:	Password:	Maintained by:
Other Website Logins (cpanel, etc.):	Purchased from:	Login:	Password:	Maintained by:
Secondary Website Domain Name:	Purchased from:	Login:	Password:	Maintained by:
Other Website Domain Name:	Purchased from:	Login:	Password:	Maintained by:
Other Website Domain Name:	Purchased from:	Login:	Password:	Maintained by:
Other Website Domain Name:	Purchased from:	Login:	Password:	Maintained by:

NEWSLETTER

Newsletter Service Link:	Login:	Password:	Maintained by:	Cost:
Newsletter Service Link:	Login:	Password:	Maintained by:	Cost:

ANTI-VIRUS / SECURITY PROGRAMS

Lifelock (or similar):	Login:	Password:	As of date:	2FA:	Notes:
Anti-Virus:	Login:	Password:	As of date:	2FA:	Notes:
Anti-Virus:	Login:	Password:	As of date:	2FA:	Notes:
VPN:	Login:	Password:	As of date:	2FA:	Notes:
Other:	Login:	Password:	As of date:	2FA:	Notes:

AUTHOR ACCOUNTS

DISTRIBUTORS / REVENUE GENERATING PLATFORMS			
Amazon Login:	Password:	2FA:	As of date:
This account is different because your one Amazon login should give you access to ACX/Audible, Amazon Ads, Author Central, KDP Bookshelf, and an Amazon Affiliate account if you have one of those. This login represents the keys to an author's Amazon castle. A great deal of damage could be done if someone who doesn't know what they're doing got into your account.			
Apple Login:	Password:	2FA:	As of date:
Kobo Login:	Password:	2FA:	As of date:
Barnes & Noble Login:	Password:	2FA:	As of date:
Kobo Login:	Password:	2FA:	As of date:
Lulu Login:	Password:	2FA:	As of date:
Other Distributor (D2D, PublishDrive, etc.):	Password:	2FA:	As of date:
Other Distributor (D2D, PublishDrive, etc.):	Password:	2FA:	As of date:
Other Distributor (D2D, PublishDrive, etc.):	Password:	2FA:	As of date:
Other Distributor (D2D, PublishDrive, etc.):	Password:	2FA:	As of date:
Other Distributor (D2D, PublishDrive, etc.):	Password:	2FA:	As of date:

NOTES

AUTHOR ACCOUNTS

CONSULTING			
Who:	For what?	How much?	Notes:
Who:	For what?	How much?	Notes:
Who:	For what?	How much?	Notes:
Who:	For what?	How much?	Notes:
Who:	For what?	How much?	Notes:
Who:	For what?	How much?	Notes:
Who:	For what?	How much?	Notes:
Who:	For what?	How much?	Notes:
Who:	For what?	How much?	Notes:

AFFILIATES			
Who:	For what?	How much?	Notes:
Who:	For what?	How much?	Notes:
Who:	For what?	How much?	Notes:
Who:	For what?	How much?	Notes:
Who:	For what?	How much?	Notes:
Who:	For what?	How much?	Notes:
Who:	For what?	How much?	Notes:
Who:	For what?	How much?	Notes:
Who:	For what?	How much?	Notes:

AUTHOR ACCOUNTS

SUBSCRIPTION SERVICES - PATREON, SUBSTACK, ETC.

Admin Login Link:	Password:	Publishing Frequency:	As of date:
Admin Login Link:	Password:	Publishing Frequency:	As of date:
Admin Login Link:	Password:	Publishing Frequency:	As of date:
Admin Login Link:	Password:	Publishing Frequency:	As of date:
Admin Login Link:	Password:	Publishing Frequency:	As of date:

DIRECT SALES PLATFORMS - SHOPIFY, ETC.

Platform & Login Link:	Password:	2FA:	As of date:
Platform & Login Link:	Password:	2FA:	As of date:
Platform & Login Link:	Password:	2FA:	As of date:
Platform & Login Link:	Password:	2FA:	As of date:

CROWDFUNDING PLATFORMS - KICKSTARTER, BACKERKIT, ETC

Platform & Login Link:	Password:	How you use this service:	2FA:	As of date:
Platform & Login Link:	Password:	How you use this service:	2FA:	As of date:
Platform & Login Link:	Password:	How you use this service:	2FA:	As of date:
Platform & Login Link:	Password:	How you use this service:	2FA:	As of date:

AUTHOR SERVICES

These can include BookFunnel, BookReport, ProWriting Aid, Adobe, Canva, and all those services you pay monthly or annually. As of writing this book, I have AutoCrit (lifetime), BookFunnel, BookReport, DocuSign, Wufoo (forms), AppSumo, GeniUs Link, SurveyMonkey, Adobe, ModFarms Design (website plus monthly recurring), three paid assistants, Patreon, Microsoft (cloud storage), Apple (cloud storage), and Dropbox (cloud storage).

Service:	Login:	Password
Paid: ☐ Monthly ☐ Annually	Payment Method:	2FA:	As of Date:
Notes:		

Service:	Login:	Password
Paid: ☐ Monthly ☐ Annually	Payment Method:	2FA:	As of Date:
Notes:		

Service:	Login:	Password
Paid: ☐ Monthly ☐ Annually	Payment Method:	2FA:	As of Date:
Notes:		

Service:	Login:	Password
Paid: ☐ Monthly ☐ Annually	Payment Method:	2FA:	As of Date:
Notes:		

AUTHOR SERVICES

Service:	Login:	Password

Paid: ☐ Monthly ☐ Annually	Payment Method:	2FA:	As of Date:

Notes:

Service:	Login:	Password

Paid: ☐ Monthly ☐ Annually	Payment Method:	2FA:	As of Date:

Notes:

Service:	Login:	Password

Paid: ☐ Monthly ☐ Annually	Payment Method:	2FA:	As of Date:

Notes:

Service:	Login:	Password

Paid: ☐ Monthly ☐ Annually	Payment Method:	2FA:	As of Date:

Notes:

Service:	Login:	Password

Paid: ☐ Monthly ☐ Annually	Payment Method:	2FA:	As of Date:

Notes:

AUTHOR SERVICES

Service:	Login:	Password
Paid: ☐ Monthly ☐ Annually	Payment Method:	2FA:	As of Date:
Notes:			

Service:	Login:	Password
Paid: ☐ Monthly ☐ Annually	Payment Method:	2FA:	As of Date:
Notes:			

Service:	Login:	Password
Paid: ☐ Monthly ☐ Annually	Payment Method:	2FA:	As of Date:
Notes:			

Service:	Login:	Password
Paid: ☐ Monthly ☐ Annually	Payment Method:	2FA:	As of Date:
Notes:			

Service:	Login:	Password
Paid: ☐ Monthly ☐ Annually	Payment Method:	2FA:	As of Date:
Notes:			

AUTHOR SERVICES

Service:	Login:	Password
Paid: ☐ Monthly ☐ Annually	Payment Method:	2FA:	As of Date:
Notes:		

Service:	Login:	Password
Paid: ☐ Monthly ☐ Annually	Payment Method:	2FA:	As of Date:
Notes:		

Service:	Login:	Password
Paid: ☐ Monthly ☐ Annually	Payment Method:	2FA:	As of Date:
Notes:		

Service:	Login:	Password
Paid: ☐ Monthly ☐ Annually	Payment Method:	2FA:	As of Date:
Notes:		

Service:	Login:	Password
Paid: ☐ Monthly ☐ Annually	Payment Method:	2FA:	As of Date:
Notes:		

AUTHOR SERVICES

Service:	Login:	Password
Paid: ☐ Monthly ☐ Annually	Payment Method:	2FA:	As of Date:
Notes:		

Service:	Login:	Password
Paid: ☐ Monthly ☐ Annually	Payment Method:	2FA:	As of Date:
Notes:		

Service:	Login:	Password
Paid: ☐ Monthly ☐ Annually	Payment Method:	2FA:	As of Date:
Notes:		

Service:	Login:	Password
Paid: ☐ Monthly ☐ Annually	Payment Method:	2FA:	As of Date:
Notes:		

Service:	Login:	Password
Paid: ☐ Monthly ☐ Annually	Payment Method:	2FA:	As of Date:
Notes:		

AUTHOR SERVICES

Service:	Login:	Password

Paid: ☐ Monthly ☐ Annually	Payment Method:	2FA:	As of Date:

Notes:

Service:	Login:	Password

Paid: ☐ Monthly ☐ Annually	Payment Method:	2FA:	As of Date:

Notes:

Service:	Login:	Password

Paid: ☐ Monthly ☐ Annually	Payment Method:	2FA:	As of Date:

Notes:

Service:	Login:	Password

Paid: ☐ Monthly ☐ Annually	Payment Method:	2FA:	As of Date:

Notes:

Service:	Login:	Password

Paid: ☐ Monthly ☐ Annually	Payment Method:	2FA:	As of Date:

Notes:

IMPORTANT PEOPLE

IMPORTANT PEOPLE

This section is for recording the details of the people who are instrumental in your writing business. It's best to keep this information updated in a spreadsheet.

Spreadsheet – An Author's Legacy - https://geni.us/AnAuthorsLegacy

You'll have to download the file to the type of your choice, like Google Sheets or Excel. This file can only be viewed via Google. Also, please do not share this spreadsheet – it is exclusively for the use of those who bought this planner.

PAID ASSISTANTS: KNOWS AT LEAST PART OF MY BUSINESS			
Name:	Email:	Phone:	Other ways to contact:
Name:	Email:	Phone:	Other ways to contact:
Name:	Email:	Phone:	Other ways to contact:

EDITORS				
Name:	Email	Phone:	Pay Rate:	Other ways to contact:
Name:	Email	Phone:	Pay Rate:	Other ways to contact:
Name:	Email	Phone:	Pay Rate:	Other ways to contact:

COVER ARTISTS			
Name:	Email	Phone:	Other ways to contact:
Name:	Email	Phone:	Other ways to contact:
Name:	Email	Phone:	Other ways to contact:
Name:	Email	Phone:	Other ways to contact:
Name:	Email	Phone:	Other ways to contact:

IMPORTANT PEOPLE

CO-AUTHORS/COLLABORATORS - PAID ON A REGULAR BASIS FOR JOINT SALES

Name:	Email:	Phone:	Other ways to contact:
Co-Authored Publications:		Contract Terms - Share % and Frequency	Duration of Contract:

Name:	Email:	Phone:	Other ways to contact:
Co-Authored Publications:		Contract Terms - Share % and Frequency	Duration of Contract:

NOTES

IMPORTANT PEOPLE

CO-AUTHORS/COLLABORATORS - PAID ON A REGULAR BASIS FOR JOINT SALES

Name:	Email:	Phone:	Other ways to contact:

Co-Authored Publications:	Contract Terms - Share % and Frequency	Duration of Contract:

Name:	Email:	Phone:	Other ways to contact:

Co-Authored Publications:	Contract Terms - Share % and Frequency	Duration of Contract:

Name:	Email:	Phone:	Other ways to contact:

Co-Authored Publications:	Contract Terms - Share % and Frequency	Duration of Contract:

NOTES

IMPORTANT PEOPLE

CO-AUTHORS/COLLABORATORS - PAID ON A REGULAR BASIS FOR JOINT SALES

Name:	Email:	Phone:	Other ways to contact:
Co-Authored Publications:		Contract Terms - Share % and Frequency	Duration of Contract:

Name:	Email:	Phone:	Other ways to contact:
Co-Authored Publications:		Contract Terms - Share % and Frequency	Duration of Contract:

Name:	Email:	Phone:	Other ways to contact:
Co-Authored Publications:		Contract Terms - Share % and Frequency	Duration of Contract:

NOTES

IMPORTANT PEOPLE

CO-AUTHORS/COLLABORATORS - PAID ON A REGULAR BASIS FOR JOINT SALES

Name:	Email:	Phone:	Other ways to contact:
Co-Authored Publications:		Contract Terms - Share % and Frequency	Duration of Contract:

Name:	Email:	Phone:	Other ways to contact:
Co-Authored Publications:		Contract Terms - Share % and Frequency	Duration of Contract:

Name:	Email:	Phone:	Other ways to contact:
Co-Authored Publications:		Contract Terms - Share % and Frequency	Duration of Contract:

NOTES

IMPORTANT PEOPLE

CO-AUTHORS/COLLABORATORS - PAID ON A REGULAR BASIS FOR JOINT SALES

Name:	Email:	Phone:	Other ways to contact:
Co-Authored Publications:		Contract Terms - Share % and Frequency	Duration of Contract:

Name:	Email:	Phone:	Other ways to contact:
Co-Authored Publications:		Contract Terms - Share % and Frequency	Duration of Contract:

Name:	Email:	Phone:	Other ways to contact:
Co-Authored Publications:		Contract Terms - Share % and Frequency	Duration of Contract:

NOTES

IMPORTANT PEOPLE

CO-AUTHORS/COLLABORATORS - PAID ON A REGULAR BASIS FOR JOINT SALES

Name:	Email:	Phone:	Other ways to contact:
Co-Authored Publications:		Contract Terms - Share % and Frequency	Duration of Contract:

Name:	Email:	Phone:	Other ways to contact:
Co-Authored Publications:		Contract Terms - Share % and Frequency	Duration of Contract:

Name:	Email:	Phone:	Other ways to contact:
Co-Authored Publications:		Contract Terms - Share % and Frequency	Duration of Contract:

NOTES

IMPORTANT PEOPLE

CO-AUTHORS/COLLABORATORS - PAID ON A REGULAR BASIS FOR JOINT SALES

Name:	Email:	Phone:	Other ways to contact:
Co-Authored Publications:		Contract Terms - Share % and Frequency	Duration of Contract:

Name:	Email:	Phone:	Other ways to contact:
Co-Authored Publications:		Contract Terms - Share % and Frequency	Duration of Contract:

Name:	Email:	Phone:	Other ways to contact:
Co-Authored Publications:		Contract Terms - Share % and Frequency	Duration of Contract:

NOTES

IMPORTANT PEOPLE

FRIENDS WHO KNOW AT LEAST PART OF MY BUSINESS			
Name:	Email	Phone:	Other ways to contact:
Name:	Email	Phone:	Other ways to contact:
Name:	Email	Phone:	Other ways to contact:
Name:	Email	Phone:	Other ways to contact:
Name:	Email	Phone:	Other ways to contact:
Name:	Email	Phone:	Other ways to contact:
Name:	Email	Phone:	Other ways to contact:
Name:	Email	Phone:	Other ways to contact:
Name:	Email	Phone:	Other ways to contact:
Name:	Email	Phone:	Other ways to contact:
Name:	Email	Phone:	Other ways to contact:
Name:	Email	Phone:	Other ways to contact:
Name:	Email	Phone:	Other ways to contact:
Name:	Email	Phone:	Other ways to contact:

NOTES

IMPORTANT PEOPLE

ALL OTHER IMPORTANT PEOPLE TO BE NOTIFIED UPON MY DEATH			
Name:	Email	Phone:	Other ways to contact:
Name:	Email	Phone:	Other ways to contact:
Name:	Email	Phone:	Other ways to contact:
Name:	Email	Phone:	Other ways to contact:
Name:	Email	Phone:	Other ways to contact:
Name:	Email	Phone:	Other ways to contact:
Name:	Email	Phone:	Other ways to contact:
Name:	Email	Phone:	Other ways to contact:
Name:	Email	Phone:	Other ways to contact:
Name:	Email	Phone:	Other ways to contact:
Name:	Email	Phone:	Other ways to contact:
Name:	Email	Phone:	Other ways to contact:
Name:	Email	Phone:	Other ways to contact:
Name:	Email	Phone:	Other ways to contact:

NOTES

IMPORTANT PEOPLE

ALL OTHER IMPORTANT PEOPLE TO BE NOTIFIED UPON MY DEATH			
Name:	Email	Phone:	Other ways to contact:
Name:	Email	Phone:	Other ways to contact:
Name:	Email	Phone:	Other ways to contact:
Name:	Email	Phone:	Other ways to contact:
Name:	Email	Phone:	Other ways to contact:
Name:	Email	Phone:	Other ways to contact:
Name:	Email	Phone:	Other ways to contact:
Name:	Email	Phone:	Other ways to contact:
Name:	Email	Phone:	Other ways to contact:
Name:	Email	Phone:	Other ways to contact:
Name:	Email	Phone:	Other ways to contact:
Name:	Email	Phone:	Other ways to contact:
Name:	Email	Phone:	Other ways to contact:
Name:	Email	Phone:	Other ways to contact:

NOTES

IMPORTANT PEOPLE

ALL OTHER IMPORTANT PEOPLE TO BE NOTIFIED UPON MY DEATH			
Name:	Email	Phone:	Other ways to contact:
Name:	Email	Phone:	Other ways to contact:
Name:	Email	Phone:	Other ways to contact:
Name:	Email	Phone:	Other ways to contact:
Name:	Email	Phone:	Other ways to contact:
Name:	Email	Phone:	Other ways to contact:
Name:	Email	Phone:	Other ways to contact:
Name:	Email	Phone:	Other ways to contact:
Name:	Email	Phone:	Other ways to contact:
Name:	Email	Phone:	Other ways to contact:
Name:	Email	Phone:	Other ways to contact:
Name:	Email	Phone:	Other ways to contact:
Name:	Email	Phone:	Other ways to contact:
Name:	Email	Phone:	Other ways to contact:

NOTES

IMPORTANT PEOPLE

ALL OTHER IMPORTANT PEOPLE TO BE NOTIFIED UPON MY DEATH			
Name:	Email	Phone:	Other ways to contact:
Name:	Email	Phone:	Other ways to contact:
Name:	Email	Phone:	Other ways to contact:
Name:	Email	Phone:	Other ways to contact:
Name:	Email	Phone:	Other ways to contact:
Name:	Email	Phone:	Other ways to contact:
Name:	Email	Phone:	Other ways to contact:
Name:	Email	Phone:	Other ways to contact:
Name:	Email	Phone:	Other ways to contact:
Name:	Email	Phone:	Other ways to contact:
Name:	Email	Phone:	Other ways to contact:
Name:	Email	Phone:	Other ways to contact:
Name:	Email	Phone:	Other ways to contact:
Name:	Email	Phone:	Other ways to contact:

NOTES

IMPORTANT PEOPLE

ALL OTHER IMPORTANT PEOPLE TO BE NOTIFIED UPON MY DEATH			
Name:	Email	Phone:	Other ways to contact:
Name:	Email	Phone:	Other ways to contact:
Name:	Email	Phone:	Other ways to contact:
Name:	Email	Phone:	Other ways to contact:
Name:	Email	Phone:	Other ways to contact:
Name:	Email	Phone:	Other ways to contact:
Name:	Email	Phone:	Other ways to contact:
Name:	Email	Phone:	Other ways to contact:
Name:	Email	Phone:	Other ways to contact:
Name:	Email	Phone:	Other ways to contact:
Name:	Email	Phone:	Other ways to contact:
Name:	Email	Phone:	Other ways to contact:
Name:	Email	Phone:	Other ways to contact:
Name:	Email	Phone:	Other ways to contact:

NOTES

IMPORTANT PEOPLE

ALL OTHER IMPORTANT PEOPLE TO BE NOTIFIED UPON MY DEATH			
Name:	Email	Phone:	Other ways to contact:
Name:	Email	Phone:	Other ways to contact:
Name:	Email	Phone:	Other ways to contact:
Name:	Email	Phone:	Other ways to contact:
Name:	Email	Phone:	Other ways to contact:
Name:	Email	Phone:	Other ways to contact:
Name:	Email	Phone:	Other ways to contact:
Name:	Email	Phone:	Other ways to contact:
Name:	Email	Phone:	Other ways to contact:
Name:	Email	Phone:	Other ways to contact:
Name:	Email	Phone:	Other ways to contact:
Name:	Email	Phone:	Other ways to contact:
Name:	Email	Phone:	Other ways to contact:
Name:	Email	Phone:	Other ways to contact:

NOTES

EMAIL ACCOUNTS

EMAIL

Email is a whole different hydra for an active author. If for some reason, you suddenly couldn't get on your email, because you passed away or became incapacitated, then what happens?

If you don't use it, you lose it. There are too many different email providers to list but generally, they'll terminate your account and delete all your information if you aren't actively using your email. In your daily life and business, you probably send an email or two from various accounts every day, maybe log in to check certain accounts and it's all good.

But your executor and your literary executor! As they try to recreate the building blocks of your business, they'll need access to these accounts so they don't miss any important emails like a quality issue, payment bounce, or royalties that need sent along, with a bazillion other reasons why an author gets emails.

Catalogue and categorize your emails. Which ones have two-factor authentication via your phone or another email? So many interworking parts that are seamless to you but will be problematic for anyone else, unless your working computer and phone were co-located with the executor. (That won't always be the case.)

PERSONAL EMAIL ACCOUNTS				
Link:	Login:	Password:	2FA:	As of date:
Link:	Login:	Password:	2FA:	As of date:
Link:	Login:	Password:	2FA:	As of date:
Link:	Login:	Password:	2FA:	As of date:
Link:	Login:	Password:	2FA:	As of date:
Link:	Login:	Password:	2FA:	As of date:

NOTES

EMAIL

BUSINESS EMAIL ACCOUNTS				
Link:	Login:	Password:	2FA:	As of date:
Link:	Login:	Password:	2FA:	As of date:
Link:	Login:	Password:	2FA:	As of date:
Link:	Login:	Password:	2FA:	As of date:
Link:	Login:	Password:	2FA:	As of date:
Link:	Login:	Password:	2FA:	As of date:
Link:	Login:	Password:	2FA:	As of date:
Link:	Login:	Password:	2FA:	As of date:
Link:	Login:	Password:	2FA:	As of date:
Link:	Login:	Password:	2FA:	As of date:

NOTES

EMAIL

BUSINESS EMAIL ACCOUNTS

Link:	Login:	Password:	2FA:	As of date:
Link:	Login:	Password:	2FA:	As of date:
Link:	Login:	Password:	2FA:	As of date:
Link:	Login:	Password:	2FA:	As of date:
Link:	Login:	Password:	2FA:	As of date:
Link:	Login:	Password:	2FA:	As of date:
Link:	Login:	Password:	2FA:	As of date:
Link:	Login:	Password:	2FA:	As of date:
Link:	Login:	Password:	2FA:	As of date:
Link:	Login:	Password:	2FA:	As of date:

NOTES

NO HEIRS

WHAT IF YOU DON'T HAVE ANY HEIRS?

1. Create a private foundation, which would then offer grants to charities. They are funded by tax-deductible donations.

2. Create a charitable remainder trust. You'll have to go through an estate planning attorney to set this up. The trust will do what you tell them to, such as charitable contributions, donations to the local children's park, whatever. The sky is the limit.

3. Leave your estate to a charity—contact the charity; they'll know what you need to do)

4. Leave your estate to a corporation

5. Leave your estate to a friend/favorite delivery person/neighbor/anyone you would like. You just need to identify them so your executor can find the correct beneficiary after your passing for notification purposes.

Entity to receive your estate:	Share (%):
Address / Contact Info:	

Entity to receive your estate:	Share (%):
Address / Contact Info:	

If you don't have a will and don't have direct heirs, the State will do their best to find any relative. If they find one, they'll probably get the remainder of your estate. If the State can find no living relatives, then the State will probably take your estate. You paid taxes on the money, so this isn't optimal. The State has already taken their cut of your wealth. Give it to someone or something.

WHAT IF YOU DON'T HAVE ANY HEIRS?

Use this page and the next to record any questions you may have for a legal professional regarding the question of who receives your estate.

WHAT IF YOU DON'T HAVE ANY HEIRS?

WORKS IN PROGRESS

YOUR WORKS IN PROGRESS

You're working on a book or story and it's not quite finished when you pass to the great beyond. Of course you are, because you're an author who is always working on something. What happens to your work in progress (WIP)?

Your literary executor finds someone to finish it, and then the literary executor publishes it under the estate account managing your distributors. Throw a cover on that baby (cover artists are listed above under People...), add in a blurb, get it edited (editor is listed above under People...), and publish it. Then send an email to the author's newsletter list. It is that easy, since you will have already taken control of the IP.

How do you finish a title that is somewhere short of The End? Author friends. Ask if someone would be willing to finish the latest work. You might be surprised at who will step up. If no one, then you can publish it as it is—unfinished and let the readers fill in the blanks.

What about other IP? When Frank Roderus, an award-winning Western author passed away, his estate found three and a half post-apocalyptic books on his computer. No one knew they existed, and that wasn't his genre. So I jumped in and finished the series, re-writing the first few books (just a little) and finishing book four, then writing books five through eight to complete the series. I make a little money off that series, but I did it as a favor to a friend. It was great to see how a Western author gripped readers with folksy language and a smooth flow.

If the literary executor has not yet taken over because a book was ready and on pre-order, then it becomes even more critical to keep those accounts open so they can receive the payout from the pre-order sales. Never mess up a pre-order. Let it ride!

And reap the rewards.

Use this space to record any questions you may have for a legal professional regarding the publishing of your works in progress.

_____

_____

_____

_____

YOUR WORKS IN PROGRESS

WORKS IN PROGRESS

| Working Title: | Series or Universe: | Folder Location on Device: |
|---|---|---|али

Any Pre-Paid Assets:

Expected Length:	Genre/Sub-Genre:

Share your inspiration/vision/plan for this story. What would it mean to you? To your readers? Other notes:

___

Working Title:	Series or Universe:	Folder Location on Device:

Any Pre-Paid Assets:

Expected Length:	Genre/Sub-Genre:

Share your inspiration/vision/plan for this story. What would it mean to you? To your readers? Other notes:

YOUR WORKS IN PROGRESS

WORKS IN PROGRESS

Working Title:	Series or Universe:	Folder Location on Device:
Any Pre-Paid Assets:		
Expected Length:	Genre/Sub-Genre:	

Share your inspiration/vision/plan for this story. What would it mean to you? To your readers? Other notes:

_____
_____
_____
_____
_____
_____
_____
_____
_____
_____

Working Title:	Series or Universe:	Folder Location on Device:
Any Pre-Paid Assets:		
Expected Length:	Genre/Sub-Genre:	

Share your inspiration/vision/plan for this story. What would it mean to you? To your readers? Other notes:

_____
_____
_____
_____
_____
_____
_____
_____
_____
_____

YOUR WORKS IN PROGRESS

WORKS IN PROGRESS

Working Title:	Series or Universe:	Folder Location on Device:

Any Pre-Paid Assets:

Expected Length:	Genre/Sub-Genre:

Share your inspiration/vision/plan for this story. What would it mean to you? To your readers? Other notes:

___

Working Title:	Series or Universe:	Folder Location on Device:

Any Pre-Paid Assets:

Expected Length:	Genre/Sub-Genre:

Share your inspiration/vision/plan for this story. What would it mean to you? To your readers? Other notes:

YOUR WORKS IN PROGRESS

WORKS IN PROGRESS

Working Title:	Series or Universe:	Folder Location on Device:
Any Pre-Paid Assets:		
Expected Length:	Genre/Sub-Genre:	

Share your inspiration/vision/plan for this story. What would it mean to you? To your readers? Other notes:
_____
_____
_____
_____
_____
_____
_____
_____
_____
_____

Working Title:	Series or Universe:	Folder Location on Device:
Any Pre-Paid Assets:		
Expected Length:	Genre/Sub-Genre:	

Share your inspiration/vision/plan for this story. What would it mean to you? To your readers? Other notes:
_____
_____
_____
_____
_____
_____
_____
_____
_____
_____

YOUR WORKS IN PROGRESS

WORKS IN PROGRESS

Working Title:	Series or Universe:	Folder Location on Device:
Any Pre-Paid Assets:		
Expected Length:	Genre/Sub-Genre:	

Share your inspiration/vision/plan for this story. What would it mean to you? To your readers? Other notes:

_____
_____
_____
_____
_____
_____
_____
_____
_____
_____
_____
_____

Working Title:	Series or Universe:	Folder Location on Device:
Any Pre-Paid Assets:		
Expected Length:	Genre/Sub-Genre:	

Share your inspiration/vision/plan for this story. What would it mean to you? To your readers? Other notes:

_____
_____
_____
_____
_____
_____
_____
_____
_____
_____
_____
_____

YOUR WORKS IN PROGRESS

WORKS IN PROGRESS

Working Title:	Series or Universe:	Folder Location on Device:
Any Pre-Paid Assets:		
Expected Length:	Genre/Sub-Genre:	

Share your inspiration/vision/plan for this story. What would it mean to you? To your readers? Other notes:
___
___
___
___
___
___
___
___
___
___

Working Title:	Series or Universe:	Folder Location on Device:
Any Pre-Paid Assets:		
Expected Length:	Genre/Sub-Genre:	

Share your inspiration/vision/plan for this story. What would it mean to you? To your readers? Other notes:
___
___
___
___
___
___
___
___
___
___

OVERSEAS RULES

Overseas Rules for Your Will & Estate

No matter which country you live in, having a full accounting of your estate is critical, which is what the previous sections of this book are all about. Here's some specific country guidance for various places around the world. This research was conducted in September 2024. These resources seemed to be the most thorough places for explanations.

Guidance for crafting a will in the UK:

From the website - https://geni.us/UKWills

I requested permission from Age UK to use their information and they recommended a link since that way, whatever is on their site is the most up to date. Go to that link and read what I would have put in here. It's good information and mirrors 99% of what we have in the U.S. with the exception of how probate is handled, inheritance tax, and asset distribution which you can make secretly via a Letter of Wishes. But only the will is legally binding, so if you want to make sure a beneficiary gets something specific, put it in the will proper.

Guidance for crafting a will in Australia:
https://geni.us/AusWills

Guidance for crafting a will in New Zealand:
https://geni.us/NZWills

Guidance for crafting a will in Canada:
https://geni.us/CanWills

Use this space to record any further questions you may have for a legal professional regarding your wills and estate.

_____
_____
_____
_____

RESOURCES

Spreadsheet – *An Author's Legacy* - https://geni.us/AnAuthorsLegacy

You'll have to download the file to the type of your choice, like Google Sheets or Excel. This file can only be viewed via Google. Also, please do not share this spreadsheet – it is exclusively for the use of those who bought this planner.

An Author Heir's Handbook: How to Manage an Author Estate by M.L. Ronn - https://www.amazon.com/dp/B09TDW94FD

The Author Estate Handbook: How to organize your affairs and leave a legacy by M.L. Ronn - https://www.amazon.com/gp/product/B09QNX2MMH

Estate Planning for Authors: Your Final Letter (and why you need to write it now) by M.L. Buchman - https://www.amazon.com/gp/product/1945740256/

AUTHOR'S NOTES

Thank you for buying this planner – you're doing yourself, your estate, and your heirs a great favor by being organized. You have more than you realize that must be accounted for and consolidated when you pass away. Put it all under one roof, right here.

Once again, I am a lawyer, but this is only a guide, and not legal advice. It's to help you help yourself. With the assistance of a good family planning lawyer (for your will) and a trust lawyer (if you need a trust), you'll have the peace of mind necessary to go about your everyday business. I hope you fight off the end as long as you want and that you have no regrets when you get there.

Set yourself up to win now and forever. An author's legacy can live on, long after you've joined your pets in the great dog park in the sky.

AUTHOR

CRAIG'S NONFICTION TITLES

THE SUCCESSFUL INDIE AUTHOR SERIES

Become a Successful Indie Author – https://geni.us/BecomeSuccessful
Release Strategies - https://geni.us/ReleaseStrategies
Collaborations - https://geni.us/Collaborations
Write Compelling Fiction - https://geni.us/WriteCompellingFiction
Pricing Strategies - https://geni.us/PricingStrategies
Wit and Wisdom – coming in 2025 https://geni.us/WitandWisdom

LEADERSHIP

The Leader Within - https://geni.us/LeaderWithin

See all of Craig's titles here: https://craigmartelle.com

AUDREY'S NONFICTION TITLES

Writing and Authorship Planners

The Author's Planner (dated, annual)

The Ultimate Authorship Planner (non-dated, 12 months)

The Simplicity Writing Planner

Monthly Writing Focus Planner

The Essential Book Launch Planner

Quarterly Author Growth Planner

The "What's Next?" Workbook

Find these titles and more at www.audreyhughey.com/planners

Made in United States
Troutdale, OR
07/11/2025